ADVANCE PRAISE

"*Tuesdays with Ted* was not what I expected. When his father was dying of ALS, Woody took him in and made him a part of his own busy life—it doesn't sound like a romp. But it was. With each turn, my emotions moved from wrenching empathy and welling tears to an event outrageously funny or a self-deprecating example of the author's own perceived shortcomings as a father. Then on to an extraordinary outpouring of kindness and love for an old man that came from, of all places, a sitcom's cast and crew. Russ Woody may not have meant it to be, but his book is a lovely paradigm of what the months, days and minutes with a fading loved one should be."

CANDICE BERGEN
Actor: *Book Club, The Women, Sweet Home Alabama, Carnal Knowledge, Gandhi, The Wind and the Lion, The Sand Pebbles, Boston Legal,* and *Murphy Brown*

"I laughed out loud and cried too. Thank you so much for this lovely, brave, and funny book. You have taught us all how to lovingly prepare and care for someone who is facing death."

MARSHA MASON
Actor, director: *Blume in Love, Cinderella Liberty, Frasier, Grace and Frankie, The Goodbye Girl, The Middle*

"Russ Woody and I have many things in common; we're the same age, and both raised in California. We share a love for comedy and drama in our show business careers, and both had a challenging relationship with our mothers. We live near each other, and would see each other frequently when he visited his dad's home—just a couple doors down from the house we used on *Malcolm in the Middle*. Russ's book is sneaky good. At first you think it's an inside look at his life in show business, but soon you realize that it's a rich story of love, friendship, and devotion. I really hate memoirs that just list all the fortunate things that happened in a person's life...they're boring. But Russ takes the reader through his emotional journey. His hopes and his insecurities. His desire to get every last valuable moment with his dad before he succumbs to the inevitable disease of ALS. Russ's ability to so artfully describe his relationship with his dad over the long, slow goodbye tugs at your heart, makes you laugh, and affirms your faith in humanity."

BRYAN CRANSTON
Actor, writer, director: *Trumbo, Malcolm in the Middle, Breaking Bad*

"Seeing Woody each week, seeing his strength and courage in the face of his great struggle was an inspiration to all of us at Becker. He gave us a lesson on life. He taught us to embrace the time we have, to love those we love."

TED DANSON
Actor, author: *Becker, Cheers, Curb Your Enthusiasm, Damages, Fargo, The Good Place, The Orville,* author of *Oceana: Our Endangered Oceans And What We Can Do To Save Them*

"*Tuesdays with Ted* is the story of fathers and sons (with an occasional appearance by a cat). Russ Woody has told his very personal story with humor, intelligence and, most importantly, love. I'm still laughing and crying."

TOM FONTANA
Writer, producer: *Homicide: Life on the Street, Oz, St. Elsewhere, Tattingers, The Wire*

"Russ Woody's father has touched many lives, from his family to Ted Danson. And I guarantee—you. *Tuesdays with Ted* is a heartfelt, funny and deeply personal account of a courageous man, beautifully told by his loving son. This is more than a book; it's a gift."

KEN LEVINE
Emmy-winning writer, producer: *M*A*S*H*, *Cheers*, *Frasier*, and *The Simpsons*, among many others

"In Russ Woody's *Tuesdays with Ted*, his father's terminal ALS diagnosis sets off an unexpected chain reaction of love and generosity in, of all places, Hollywood and the TV industry. Equal parts hilarious and heartbreaking, it's not only a love letter to his father, it's a celebration of life, and the boundless kindness humans can be capable of, even in the bleakest of circumstances."

ALAN BALL
Writer, director, producer: *American Beauty*, *Six Feet Under*, *True Blood*, *Grace Under Fire*, *Cybill*

"*Tuesdays with Ted* belongs alongside Phillip Roth's *Patrimony* and Billy Crystal's *700 Sundays* in its expression of love for those who loved us first. I had always known Russ Woody as a writer whose work was funny with heart. But in *Tuesdays with Ted* he has done the opposite—written a most passionate memoir that will make you laugh as well. A must-read for anyone who has ever had a parent. I also wanted to smack him for writing something I wished I'd written."

ALAN ZWEIBEL
Writer, author: *Saturday Night Live*, Thurber Prize winning *The Other Shulman*

TUESDAYS WITH TED

RUSS WOODY

TUESDAYS WITH TED

*An uplifting, heartbreaking, occasionally funny story
about an old man with ALS, a sitcom, its star and
just enough time for a son to say goodbye*

Wyatt-MacKenzie Publishing
DEADWOOD, OREGON

Why the title?

Tuesdays with Ted is a tongue-in-cheek salute to Mitch Albom's wonderful book *Tuesdays with Morrie.* It wasn't the intended title until a few parallels became obvious.

Tuesdays with Ted

*An uplifting, heartbreaking, occasionally funny story
about an old man with ALS, a sitcom, its star and
just enough time for a son to say good-bye*

Russ Woody

ISBN: 978-1-948018-58-6

Library of Congress Control Number: 2019941104

Wyatt-MacKenzie Publishing
DEADWOOD, OREGON

www.WyattMacKenzie.com

Requests for permission or further information should be addressed to:
Wyatt-MacKenzie Publishing
15115 Highway 36, Deadwood, Oregon 97430

Printed in the United States of America.

DEDICATION

This book was written for my sons Henry and Joe, so they might better understand what was going on around them when they were too young to fully grasp its meaning.

They knew their grandfather was dying, but they couldn't know the extent of the love their father had for him.

It is a love that is very much alive still in my love for both of them.

"My strength is made perfect in weakness."
II Corinthians. XII 9

Woody and me, circa 1966. This photo was taken an evening after 6 p.m., as is evident by the post-6 p.m.-Highball.

Contents

FOREWORD

It started with an Instant Message on Facebook. Russ Woody, whom I hadn't even thought about in the twenty-seven years that had passed since we worked together on an alleged comedy series called *Good Sports*, wanted to know if I would read the galleys of his new book and possibly give him a blurb for its cover.

I remember liking Russ. And had been a big fan of his work on some of the best sitcoms in the history of television. And since I was in search of something, anything to distract me from my own projects whose deadlines were bearing down on me, I said, "Sure."

So I gave him my home address figuring that since we lived on opposite coasts the chances of him dropping by unexpectedly in search of a hot meal were slim. And when the book arrived, the envelope sat on my desk for about a week while I made believe that playing Words With Friends and watching reruns of *Law & Order: SVU* were actually cutting into my own workload. Eventually I grew tired of this self-delusion, opened the envelope, started reading *Tuesdays with Ted* and I was hooked.

Comedy writers, as a lot, look at the world from angles that seek out the funny in our existences. Yes, to make audiences laugh. But also as a personal salve for the pain brought by any unexpected turns that show up in our own existences. *Tuesdays with Ted*—about Russ's dad's bout with ALS while Russ was a writer on *Becker*—

is one of those books whose theme resonates while you are reading it and lingers long after you've finished.

The Ted in the title is Ted Danson and this remarkable memoir chronicles the way he and the entire cast and crew of *Becker* embraced Russ's dad when it was Russ's turn to be a parent to his father. When Russ, while dealing with a story that would not have a happy ending was given a blessed opportunity to pay back. Heal wounds. And sum up with the man everyone affectionately called "Woody."

Not since I read Phillip Roth's *Patrimony* and had a hand in collaborating with Billy Crystal on his play *700 Sundays* have I been so affected by the expression of love for someone who loved us first. Read this book. Change the names and places and personalize it so the story becomes your story. That's the beauty of comedy writing. When done properly, it will make you laugh. When done expertly as Russ had done here, it will also make you hug someone you don't want to let go.

ALAN ZWEIBEL
Original *Saturday Night Live* writer, Thurber Prize winning author of *The Other Shulman*

PROLOGUE
The Man in the Tux

Ted Danson stood in the strident glare of the Beverly Hilton's stage lights, shading his eyes to search for my father amidst the sea of several hundred tuxedos and glittering evening gowns that filled the hotel's expansive dining room. He was accepting an award from the Muscular Dystrophy Association for an episode of *Becker*, an episode I'd written about my dad.

Ted called into the microphone, "Woody?"

From a large table near the back railing of the main floor, my father put his hand in the air and waved as though to a distant ship. He had always been called by his last name, deciding early on it was preferable to his other two names: Claude and Herman.

"Yes, I see you raising your hand," the actor said, as a few hundred faces turned to find Woody in the audience. He was handsome, my dad, movie star handsome when he was younger, with still a full head of sturdy white hair and steel blue eyes. He had arrived at the Beverly Hilton that evening by limousine, the first he'd ever ridden in, donning a jet-black tuxedo, the first he'd ever worn.

Emotion edged its way into Ted's words, as he put a hand to his heart and leaned again into the microphone. "You make me miss my daddy."

Beneath the dining room's flowing crystal chandeliers, the only sounds made came from wait and bus people, moving from table to table like roving cats, removing thick china and glinting silverware. My father's sister, sitting next to him, reached over and touched his arm. My wife, on the other side of him, rested a gentle hand on his shoulder. At the same time, a small wave of self-conscious laughter rippled through the audience, as many became aware of themselves; women—who sought tissues from purses to wipe away emerging tears—and men struggling to deny needing the same.

I'd been writing and producing television shows, mostly sitcoms, for nearly twenty years, but only recently had my father seen much of my world. Now he was in the middle of it, and on this night, the object of it.

"It's a joy for all of us to be here to honor you," Ted said to him across the massive room. "You've made our year at *Becker* really special, Woody."

It was a moment in time that will never leave my heart. But there were more moments to come that evening, more that would shine brightly; moments that, ultimately, had to be clutched and pulled close, committed to memory and held as floating beacons amidst the 17 short months I was able to spend with my dad while he was dying.

He was diagnosed in the spring of 2001 with amyotrophic lateral sclerosis, ALS—Lou Gehrig's disease—a fatal illness that gradually paralyzes its victim. Three days after his diagnosis, my mother died unexpectedly from complications of a bleeding ulcer.

They'd been married 58 years.

And while my father's life was winding down, with the death of my mother, it was also—it has to be said—opening up. He had always been easy going, gregarious, fun to be with; qualities that perhaps fueled my mother's emotional insecurities. Insecurities that, in turn, drove her to feel threatened by his relationships with just about everyone, including me. And that's what would be both so sweet and heartbreaking about the months that were to follow—I was finally able to spend all the time I wanted with my dad, but *time* was something we had little of.

As a result, the time we did spend together presented a rarified window, a sliver of light that flashed across the sky like the wing of a Blue Angel. I couldn't stop the spinning clock, couldn't steal more time, but I could cling to those moments we had. To be sure, most of them were more prosaic than profound; they were the everyday dribble of banalities that are hardly noticed until due to expire. Watching TV, I would turn and quietly study him, the familiar wrinkles of his hands, the crappy Timex at his wrist, the faded tattoo above it on his forearm: an eagle atop the U.S.M.C.'s globe and anchor, now a fading image that I had traced a million times when I was small and sitting on his lap. I found myself secretly eye-balling him like he was a curious stranger in the next booth of a diner—the crease of his ear, the lines of his forehead, the dark hair of his eyebrows—I soaked it in, as much as I could, knowing that he, like his tattoo, was fading.

To be with him, to be with a parent, while he is dying, is one of the most human of experiences. It is what we are supposed to do. And while those months were difficult in myriad ways, they were also the richest and most rewarding of my life. They were, as well, chock-ablock with humor, since—as nearly any comedy writer will tell you—in the midst of great hardship, there is always funny.

Though at the time, I didn't think of the experience as an "honor," as I look back, I realize that it was an honor of the highest order.

ONE
The Phone Call

Before the black tie gala, before my mother's death, before my father's life turned on a dime, there was a phone call.

It was an evening in March, the weather was L.A. balmy, almost summerlike. My wife Catherine and I had a few friends over for drinks and dinner. Cath is Australian, and dinner parties are something Australians seem to excel at (often to an alarming degree). Australia, in case you didn't know, is a decidedly social country, where the consumption of food and beverages in groups is a mandated and weekly occurrence, most often extending into the wee hours of the morning.

Henry and Joe had been earlier put to bed, though who knows if they were asleep. Or even in bed. At five and three, sleep was not something they did on command (often popping up later in odd and unexpected places, where they would need to be captured and returned to their bedroom). As usual, everyone was gathered around the island in the kitchen where Cath was making dinner. I was preparing and serving up another round of champagne cocktails when the phone rang. I let the answering machine pick up—after all, the making of champagne cocktails is an intricate operation that requires great skill and concentration.

"Hey, Russell? It's Henry Lingam. I live down the street from your mom and dad. Need to talk to you about your mom."

I picked up. "Hello?"

"Oh, hey, Russell. Look, your dad wanted me to talk to you, 'cause he's havin' some trouble talking."

"Right."

For the past several months, my dad's speech had become noticeably slurred. We at first attributed the difficulty to loose dentures. Something that made sense to me, since he was not a particularly vain man, priding himself on bargain basement haircuts and pants bought from the shelves of hardware stores. So it was not un-reasonable to assume that he had tried to save a few bucks on dentures. Later, when we realized it wasn't his dentures, we suspected that he might have suffered a small stroke.

"So, what's going on?" I asked.

"Well, we took your mom over to Sunset Hospital down in Las Vegas. She was in quite a bit of pain. They operated right away. Seems she had a bleeding ulcer..."

It would turn out to be the beginning of the end for my mother. Complications from the bleeding ulcer and an infection after surgery—an elevated white cell count and, as it was explained to me, some of her internal organs began to stick together—ultimately combined to bring about her death a few weeks later.

At the time, my parents were living in a small town in Nevada, about 50 miles northwest of Las Vegas. Pahrump. *Why* they were living there, I couldn't tell you. It's a small, flat desert town with scattered cactus and darting lizards, where shoulder-less roads crisscross baking sand and actual tumbleweeds can be seen actually tumbling. Interestingly, Pahrump is noted mostly for being just far enough from Vegas to operate legal brothels. And there are several. Hence, on any given weekend night, the peculiar influx of limousines and Porsches, red and black, flowing into this otherwise featureless town. The other thing Pahrump is known for is Art Bell, an older gentleman who, at the time, broadcast a syndicated talk show from his home, discussing a multitude of late night conspiracies about robotic insects, aliens and micro-chipped beings living among us.

After my father's retirement from PG&E (the gas and electric company in Northern California—the one that's in all sorts of trouble these days), my parents moved frequently, often to remote and peculiar places. They'd live there for a year or two and, after no one came to visit, they'd pick up and move to another remote and peculiar place and wonder why no one was coming to visit. In reality, it was not so much the remoteness or the peculiar-ness of their domiciliary choices, as it was the feelings many of us harbored about my mother.

I flew out to Las Vegas and drove to Pahrump a couple of times in the month that my mother was hospitalized, to see her, yes, but mostly to see my dad, to help out around the house and yard, etc. *Becker* was winding down its third production season, so the workload was freeing me up to do so. Then in early April, I flew into Las Vegas and stopped by the hospital to look in on my mother for what would be the last time.

The elevator, on the way up to the ICU, smelled like a minty disease. I was sharing it with an older man in suspenders who had a hump in his back that reminded me of Marty Feldman's Igor. "What hump?" Together we silently studied the row of buttons leading up to the sixth floor. When the doors whooshed open, we were spit out onto a tile corridor that had been polished to the point of non-existence. As I made my way to the nurses' station, the ceiling's sprinklers floating far beneath my feet, I knew I would be expected to show love and support and encouragement, and the prospect of doing so mortified me. There had been too many stinging words hurled without care, too many barbs, too much abuse. So the mustering within of a sympathetic tenor always left me feeling clumsy and stupid and mostly dishonest.

At the nurses' station, I asked for Patricia Woody's room. The nurses were confused. They knew my mother as Mary. Which was her real name, but she had always told me her name was Patricia. And everyone called her Pat so, at an early age, I made the assumption and spent my youth believing that her real name was Patricia. Then, when I was in my thirties, she called, on the verge of tears: "Rusty," she said. "I have something to tell you."

"Oh. Okay."

"I should have told you sooner."

"Right, well...okay."

"I'm sorry I didn't tell you."

"Uh-huh..."

"My real name is Mary. My middle name is Jane."

Then she was crying.

I waited for more. I mean, to me, using an alternate name didn't sound all that life shattering. So I waited. But that was it. That was the source of her anguish. "Well, uh...okay," I said. "Thank you for sharing that." I was trying to sound sincere, compassionate; unsure if I should or shouldn't express sympathy, to say I was *sorry* to hear that her name was Mary.

Conversations with my mother were mostly awkward and almost always confusing. More often than not, I would hang up the phone after a conversation and need to take a moment to collect my thoughts, to shake off the residual bewilderment.

Around the same time, when I was in my mid-thirties, she'd sent me a box of things, kind of a "Care Package," which I'll admit *was* thoughtful. Though baffling. Inside the box was a pink paisley ceramic cat, maybe 7 inches tall, sent, I guess, because I used to have a cat. There was an old diaper that I have to assume was mine, one of my baby shoes, a chewed number two pencil and a Care Bear pencil sharpener, included because...I was a writer? Then there was a folded piece of paper with a list of professional NFL teams (never was able to figure that one out). Most baffling, however, was a small toy truck. A Monster Truck, maybe two inches long, green, with thick black tires. I was able to figure out the possible logic behind most of the box's contents, but the Monster Truck had me stumped. I had no particular interest in trucks or toy trucks, monster or otherwise.

"So, you got the box of goodie-goodies?" she asked on the phone a few days later. She always talked like that. A characteristic that made me enormously uncomfortable as I got older. With my mother, Jewish people were always called "juicy Jews," though I'm at a loss to explain why. Gay people were called "fag-amolas." Penises were called "piddle-diddles" and "tally-whackers."

Quiche was called "hootchie-toochie lorraine." Again, I couldn't tell you why.

"Yes. Thank you," I eked out.

"It was just some things I thought you'd want to have."

"Right. Well, yes, thanks. And the truck, where'd that come from?"

"Oh, that was yours, when you were little. You used to play with that little truck all the time. All the time," she laughed.

"But...I don't think this was mine," I said, looking it over.

"Sure. You'd lie on the floor with that truck, and push it all over the living room. And you'd say, 'Udden-udden-udden.'" She laughed again.

"Okay, but I really don't think this was my truck," I said.

"Oh, it was your truck. You'd push it around and say, 'udden-udden-udden.' You just don't remember is all." (The last was said with an inflection that implied unlimited patience for a struggling and dimwitted son.)

I dropped the subject because I didn't want to challenge her grasp of what was what.

After we'd hung up and I'd collected my thoughts, I picked up the truck to toss in the trash when something occurred to me. I turned it over to check its underside for a copyright. It was made by the Mattel Company in 1986.

In 1986 I was thirty.

A few months later, I received a large opened jar of mega-vitamins with a note from her, explaining her reason for sending them: "These are for you," the note said. "They give me diarrhea."

There were not just laughable moments, of course, as all too often her emotional vicissitudes—fueled, or fueled *by*, her feelings of inadequacy—manifested themselves in vitriolic and sometimes cruel diatribes. Though, to the outside world, she was regarded—especially by those who did not know her well—as quirky and sometimes funny. As a result, I spent my late teens tortured by the gap between the hostile environment I lived in, and the lighthearted familial setting that others perceived.

From the nurses' station, I was escorted to my mother's room by a large nurse who walked with a disturbing waddle. Along the way, she said that all of the nurses just loved Mary. That Mary was so sweet and funny. That they have really been pulling for Mary.

When she led me into the room, I felt like she'd made a mistake. The woman in the bed didn't look like my mother. Her hair was shoved straight back like she'd stuck her head out the window of a fast-moving car. She was heavier than I remembered seeing her; bloated, dull, pasty. She was asleep and I was grateful for that. As the nurse squished off, I pulled up a chair to sit and look at this woman, my mother.

I was trying to muster the appropriate emotions. I mean, if this *was* her deathbed, I needed to be feeling certain things. The things one should feel at the deathbed of one's mother.

I watched the rise and fall of her chest beneath the dull blue bed sheet. Clear plastic tubes wiggled out of IV bags suspended above her, flowing down to her right arm, where the skin looked like it could be torn with a vigorous pinch.. It was bruised, her arm, from an assault of needles—purple highlights on a map of sheer velum. A bank of gadgetry hummed and beeped on the wall behind her. A little green worm snaked its way across the screen on a disinterested heart monitor. Across the room, the dark face of a silent television hung precariously overhead—suspended from the wall by a single straining metal arm—its face reflecting only the vague greenish image of a play actor sitting beside an unconscious woman.

I was trying to summon memories of those years when I was very young and loved her. She was kind to me until I was eleven; by some measures, overly attentive. There were nice memories, like when I used to hold on to the bottom of her camel-hair coat while we walked through Montgomery Ward. And I remembered coming home from school with artwork that she said she'd keep forever. I remembered sitting on her lap, playing with the wedding ring on her finger, finding comfort in the warmth of her hand. But those things, those feelings, were long ago, having atrophied and fallen away under the duress of her latter enmity. How does one reach back for a memory's emotion that has since morphed into something else? How does one reach into a mist and grasp at something that is no longer there? I couldn't summon that love for her, so how could I feel grief? I certainly felt no sorrow. I was just a guy sitting in a hospital room beside the bed of an old woman; a volunteer sitting vigil for a stranger. My emotions didn't feel appropriately significant.

And then it occurred to me why—I had *already* grieved for her. Years ago. And intensely.

In my early teens.

With the onset of my adolescence and emerging in-dependence, she felt—for her own distant and sup-pressed reasons—that I was a threat to her relationship with her husband. She responded with hostility; a hos-tility that would grow more intense as time went by. On one occasion, when I was in college, I ended a phone conversation with my father by saying, "I love you, Dad." He said, "I love you too." Apparently my mother had heard the last and, as I learned later, it was the catalyst for two days of bitter fighting between them.

In my early teens, I had little understanding of this dynamic's effect on me. Nor did I understand the loss I was feeling from her rejection. Yet, in the subsequent years, the pain of that emotional separation manifested itself in several debilitating bouts of clinical depres-sion...a condition not uncommon among those who have suffered early familial losses.

But there in the hospital room, as I looked at her in the bed—the threat of her fury, her power, now rendered limp—I felt mostly a sadness for the potential of her life, all of it squandered on misplaced fear and unnecessary choices.

As I stood to leave—convinced that I had paid what was due, that I had done my best to "feel" for my mother—another nurse entered the room. This one tall, robust, filled with a liveliness that seemed wildly out of place. "Why don't you go ahead and wake Mary," she said as she snapped the shades open and blasted the room with screaming light.

"No, no, that's okay. Let her sleep," I said, trying to sound heroic, regretting that I'd not made my move for the door seconds earlier.

"Oh, she's been sleeping all day," the nurse said with a twinkle. And before I could stop her, she was gently shaking my mother's shoulder. "Mary. Mary."

Mary's eyes slowly blinked to life.

"Look, Mary. You have a visitor." Proud of her accomplishment, the nurse turned to me like she'd suddenly brought meaning to my life. She smiled then and floated out of the room like a large evil pixie.

"Thank you," I called after her, thinly veiling my deep-seated resentment.

I turned back to my mother, as her eyes adjusted to the light of the room. When she found me, it took her a moment to register who I was. I stood there stupidly beside her bed and forced an encouraging smile. I'd felt uncomfortable touching her, and especially kissing her, since my adolescence. Ever since she started treating me differently. Still, I reached out and gently put my hand on her arm. It was soft, doughy, like a computer gel pad. She was looking at me like she knew me, but had to study the contours of my face to be sure. I smiled and said I'd heard she was doing better, which wasn't exactly a lie—they'd taken the breathing tube out earlier that day. Her eyes shifted to watch my mouth as I spoke, searching I suppose for something she couldn't find—something perhaps that wasn't there.

She wasn't speaking, in part I was told, because the breathing tube had been in her throat for the past couple of weeks.

Under her wordless gaze, time slowed to a crawl. I held her arm and heard the second hand on the industrial clock over the door separate each second into two distinct parts. "Things will be okay," I said, because I couldn't think of anything else to say. "Things will work out okay..." I was struggling for another way to say the same thing again.

She continued to look at me without speaking. She was a lost child in need, hoping I could offer salvation. That was what she wanted. Her eyes were pleading, beseeching me to save her from the present, or maybe the past—as though I could reach into the miasma of reality and twist it into something different; a new life, a new beginning, like I could break the neck of the Stygian force that was clawing at her, clutching at her, drawing her down.

I leaned over and kissed the cool skin of her forehead. But it was not so much an act of kindness, not really affection, as it was more a means of getting me out of the room. I squeezed her arm one more time, just to indicate I was about to leave, when she started to say something. Or tried to say something. Her lips moved, but there was no sound.

I looked at her, trying to imply that I understood. I told her to rest, thinking she might give up the effort.

And, again, her lips began to move, as she seemed determined to form words for me.

I leaned in to listen more closely, to watch her mouth, to understand what she was trying to say. And, slowly her lips formed soundless words.

"I'm sorry," she said.

TWO
A Funeral

We sat on the back seat of the golf cart, my son Joe and I, as it trundled over the parched grass of a military cemetery just outside of Boulder City, Nevada. The cart bumped its way past a row of granite markers. Joe's light-up sneakers stuck out over the edge of the back seat, as the dry desert air tussled his mop of blond hair. He was studying intently the dull black plastic box on my lap. "That's Grandma?" he said.

"Yeah." I lifted it. It was perhaps a foot long, five or six inches wide, the black plastic scuffed and gray in places.

"Oh."

I shook it a little and looked at him. "Not much after an entire lifetime, huh? To just end up in a little box like this?"

He thought about that a moment and looked out behind us where another golf cart and the others were following between the rows of headstones and embedded plaques. He squinted again at the box. "They burned her up?"

"Yeah."

He nodded, processing the particulars. "Can I hold her?"

"Sure," I said, and put the box gently on his lap.

He held it, sizing it up, jiggling it like I had. "It's heavy."

I thought about it. "Yeah."

My brother, Phil, was there. Nine years older than I, and half a foot shorter. With his stocky frame and thick glasses, we have never really looked like brothers. And we'd never been all that close, but we maintained a friendly relationship throughout the years. Henry Lingam, my parents' neighbor, was walking beside him. He was a robust and slender man in his early seventies, who looked like he'd still do well in a game of full-court hoops. My dad's sister, Oleta, was walking with my dad. A couple of years younger than he, she adored him— though, like many of us, found her time with him limited by my mother. Craig McCall, my best friend from college, walked on the other side of my father. He and his family lived in Las Vegas, and so had gotten to know my parents fairly well in the couple of years since "Pat" and Woody moved to Pahrump. Catherine walked with Henry, who held her hand and looked a little daunted, possibly by the thought of so many dead people beneath his feet.

My father was characteristically stoic about the sequence of events that had to be dealt with before one buries a spouse—the arrangements for cremation, the insurance issues, the personal effects, scheduling at the cemetery—all of it done with his usual sense of pragmatism, though it was all made considerably more difficult by his dwindling ability to speak.

As we gathered around the stark hole in the ground—a smattering of disparate souls beneath the punishing Nevada sun, barely enough of us to form an impressive semicircle—Joe was still holding the box with his grandmother's ashes. I took it from him and placed it in the hole, then stepped back. A small bit of dust welled up around it, as dry dirt from a mound beside it quietly sifted back into the hole and on top of the box. Each of us looked on, lost in our own thoughts. No one knew quite what to say about a woman none of us was particularly fond of.

So no one spoke.

It was, I suppose, my place, or my brother's place, to say something. But I was at a loss. There was nothing really to say about her life, except that she did it poorly. Not great fodder for a eulogy. There were a plethora of reasons for her insecurities, most of which, for obvious reasons, I was never privy to. I was told she'd had a difficult childhood. And she struggled with depression in a time when depressive illnesses were not acknowledged or treated, nor were they even recognized for their biochemical aspects. As a result, she medicated with alcohol and responded to life with anger. I suppose I could have mimicked what my father told me many times in the past, that she did the best she could. But whenever he said it—especially when I was in high school—I countered that she *didn't* do the best she could. For me, that was the point.

I knew Phil wouldn't say anything. He was not good at couching animosity, especially an accumulated lifetime's worth. Because of our age difference, my memories of him when I was growing up were limited, but I believe he was *never* treated well by our mother. (He did not have the eleven-year window that I did.)

RUSS WOODY

In fact, I cannot recall a single instance of our mother referring to him in anything but pejorative terms.

So, there we stood, looking at a pitiful plastic box in a dirt hole, sprinklers clicking out a song in the distance, the desert sun pushing down on our shoulders like God pressing us to move on. A man from the cemetery, when he realized no one had anything to say, stepped up to shovel the dirt into the hole and over the box.

And that was it.

That the culmination of my mother's life came to a handful of dispassionate observers standing around with nothing to say was perhaps the saddest testament to her time on earth. It had run its course, leaving behind only blemished memories, those too destined to grow dim and one day vanish. And, as the shovel tamped down the protrusion of dirt over her grave, I thought, what else could it have been?

As we stood there another moment, I realized my father was crying. My aunt turned and embraced him. It felt surreal. I'd never seen him cry. He had always been the ex-Marine, the indomitable bulwark who barely winced at life's harshest turns. His steady countenance was the one constant in my life; forever the pacific voice in the midst of chaos, the sturdy figure that frequently put an arm around his too-sensitive son, his emotional kid, and said, "Don't worry, Russ, we'll figure this out."

Now he was weeping, I suppose, for the good and the bad in the nearly six decades they'd spent together. And there was good. It had been there in the more peaceful periods of their relationship.

And early on.

Their decision to marry had been the result of a joke taken seriously, along with the happenstance of a battleship's mechanical problems. Like nearly every union, nearly every convergence of souls, it was a series of odd coincidences that culminated in its occurrence. In this case, perhaps, a perfect storm.

During the fall of 1943, the *USS Nevada* was scheduled to dock for two weeks in Boston. It was due then to ship out for the European theatre of the war. (This was the same battleship that was badly damaged by Japanese bombers in the attack on Pearl Harbor.) Woody was a 19-year-old Marine Corps Sergeant, assigned to one of the *Nevada's* 20 mm guns in the battle station just below the bridge of the ship.

During the ship's two-week stay in Boston, my father met my mother through another Marine who was dating a friend of my mother's. The four of them went out, and while the other two were making *serious* plans to wed, my mother and father began to joke that they too would get married. All of it, harmless jest.

At the end of two weeks, my parents said their goodbyes and that was that. But as the ship made its way out of Boston Harbor, engine trouble crippled it, and it was tugged back into port, where it would stay for another two months. In that time, my parents saw each other again, as did their friends, and near the end of those two months, the joke about getting married morphed into a small ceremony and a license from the Commonwealth of Massachusetts.

That he loved her in the beginning and perhaps at other times in their marriage, I'm sure, was true. But it was a tumultuous relationship at best, rocked more than a few times by near separations and at least one instance of his extended absence.

That, apparently, is what led to my birth.

In late 1954, he'd packed his bags and moved out. But later, he worried about having done so, worried about my brother who was eight, and I'm sure he felt the pressure of an era when divorce was social anathema. So he returned. When he did, she became pregnant in what I imagine was her way of securing the marriage. After my arrival, she saw me as a way to revitalize and fortify her role as mother and wife. Which might also explain her sudden disdain for me when I later approached puberty and sought to exert some autonomy.

As I watched my father on the other side of my mother's grave—overcome by emotion, embraced by my aunt—I felt disoriented by the very thought that he was vulnerable.

Afterwards, I watched him walking with his sister as we made our way back to the parking lot, and it struck me that, vulnerable or not, he was now mine. I had him all to myself. It was a strange feeling, exhilarating in some ways, but terrifying in others, as I realized that he was also now my responsibility. Certainly it is a natural progression, though a peculiar transformation, since, when the child must care for the parent, the parent *becomes* the child. And conversely the child must become, once and for all, the adult.

For some, this metamorphosis creeps in softly like a low-lying fog at the bank of a river, while for others it is foist upon them suddenly by a turn of events. Some are never faced with it for a variety of reasons, while still others *choose* not take part in the process, frequently as a reaction to a long-since withered or abusive relationship. Had the order of my parents' deaths been reversed, that is the choice I would have faced.

My brother Phil later chose not to take part in the time Woody had left. Not because there was animosity, not because he didn't love his father, he did. He even admired him. And he liked him. Nor was it a matter of geography; Phil lived in Salinas, a few hours away. It was something else altogether: He was, he said, not comfortable seeing his father decline.

When I learned why he'd kept his distance, I was reminded of a common complaint about the discomfort some feel with an open casket at a funeral. They'd rather "remember him the way he was." Except our dad wasn't in a casket. His mind was alive, aware, he was looking out at the world. And understanding it. But whether or not Phil's absence hurt him, I can't say. Woody was dismissive about the subject, waving it off with a gesture that implied it was not a big deal. I brought it up only once, and then let it go.

Unfortunately for Phil, what he missed was a broad spectrum of colors, a panoply of emotional richness, a crossing of worlds, extraordinary kindness, quiet bravery and tremendous love. Yes, there was heartache, but there was also great joy. Especially when Woody laughed. And though his voice lacked volume, in the months to come, he laughed often and heartily.

"Only a total stranger could ask such a question. Are there control agencies? There are only control agencies. Of course they aren't meant to find errors, in the vulgar sense of that term, since no errors occur, and even if an error does occur, as in your case, who can finally say that it is an error."

Franz Kafka, *The Castle*

THREE
The UCLA Experience

During the time my mother was in the hospital, my dad's speech was slowly descending from slurred-but-intelligible to barely understandable. His GP in Pahrump had ruled out a stroke and suggested Woody see a neurologist in Las Vegas to "rule out ALS." The neurologist ruled out everything but ALS. By then we knew what the answer was, but we made an appointment nonetheless at UCLA, where they specialize in ALS and, in fact, are world renown for their research.

Fortunately, *Becker* was on hiatus, so my days had been freed up to arrange such things. With the help again of his neighbor, my dad booked a flight from Las Vegas to Burbank. By this time, my mother had been in the hospital for three weeks, which I was thankful for since, as the logistics with my dad became more complex, her inclusion would have complicated things considerably. As it was, his booking flights, renting cars and dealing with personnel in doctors' offices was becoming just about impossible. He could no longer communicate by phone, and person-to-person interaction involved his writing things out for people who often seemed not-all-that-fond of complex ideas and reading hand-written notes.

Inside the hallowed halls of UCLA, we met with Dr. Michael Graves, a balding, bespectacled man with a calm and reassuring presence. His was a respected name in ALS research—though, as a comedy writer, it was hard not to appreciate a doctor named "Graves" who'd chosen to specialize in a terminal illness.

After a battery of tests were run, Dr. Graves came back into the exam room, perusing the paperwork on his clipboard. When he finally looked up and put the clipboard aside, he leaned against the sink's counter and informed us that, yes, it was ALS. His tone was steady, professional, with what seemed like a tinge of sympathy. Doubtless he had made the speech many times before and to people younger than my father. *Those* speeches were, I'm sure, considerably more difficult. The same news for someone in their thirties or forties, would shatter more than just one life. For some it meant going home to tell an anxious spouse and small children that their mother or father would soon grow weak and then leave them. And those families, in the months to follow, would either coalesce or fall apart.

The general prognosis for ALS is a gradual loss of motor functions, as the motor neurons between the body's muscle groups and the spinal column begin to die. The muscles become useless, lifeless. Mitch Albom explained it in *Tuesdays with Morrie*:

ALS is like a lit candle: it melts your nerves and leaves your body a pile of wax... By the end, if you are still alive, you are breathing through a tube in a hole in your throat, while your soul, perfectly awake, is imprisoned inside a limp husk, perhaps able to blink, or cluck a tongue, like something from a science fiction movie, the man frozen inside his own flesh.

Albom was describing the particular form of ALS that was affecting Morrie Schwartz, called limb onset. Woody's form of ALS was more aggressive, starting in the neck and throat (hence his declining ability to speak), called Bulbar onset. It affects the muscles of the lungs sooner than does the other type, and therefore the life-expectancy is considerably shorter. No matter, with either, the body slowly dies, while the mind continues to live. It is, in a manner of thinking, the opposite of Alzheimer's—the body goes away, while the mind stays intact.

Before Dr. Graves left the exam room, he told us that another doctor would come in to give us information about the disease, and then he would return. He shook our hands and left.

I sat down and smiled softly at my dad. He smiled back and shrugged. Then he reached over and rubbed my shoulder, as though I was the one who needed comforting. He said something that I couldn't quite make out. I asked him to say it again. He said that at least he'd gotten to live a long life.

The door opened again and another doctor came in, a woman in her forties with short abrupt hair, her arms laden with file folders and pamphlets. She introduced herself and, without fanfare, started handing us brochures and leaflets and fliers and charts and pictures that would tell us exactly all the incredible things my dad could look forward to. She seemed like an untroubled travel agent confirming for us, with colorful literature, our excellent choice of fabulous destination getaways. It was bizarre, but what amazed me—no, astounded me—was that she handed my dad, not *me,* one of the more graphic of the booklets, replete with illustrations of wilted persons in wheelchairs, a neck brace holding up a slouching head on a limp neck, a feeding tube inserted into a hole cut at the top of a stomach.

When my dad looked up from the "literature," the doctor mentioned that there were support groups we could join. Woody handed me the material and made a joke about not wanting to see any of "those type people." It wasn't a funny ha-ha joke, but I got it. He could tell from the pamphlets that the latter stages of this disease weren't pretty—so why would he want to see it ahead of time?

After we had been inundated with the visual panoply of Woody's future, the woman left; off, I suppose, to her next vacationer.

When Graves returned, he mentioned that, while there was no cure for ALS, there was an experimental Creatine program going on at the university that Woody could take part in. We, of course, jumped at the opportunity—though at the time I didn't even know what exactly Creatine was, only that it had something to do with muscle mass. We were told to come back in a couple of weeks to start the treatment, so it meant my dad would have to fly back to Nevada and then return to Los Angeles.

Still, it was fine with us.

It was all we had.

That night, I picked up chicken from Koo Koo Roo, normally a favorite of mine, though on that night, I found myself going through the motions, not tasting anything. And though Woody could still eat some solid foods, he ate very little. Cath and the boys were in Australia for a couple of weeks on their spring break from school (she teaches at a local high school). So the house felt especially empty, especially quiet. We didn't talk about his diagnosis. I suppose we were just weighing everything. I'd put the literature aside to read later. I wanted to let him forget about it.

Groundhog Day was on TV, a movie that I had loved since I'd first seen it many years earlier. Woody had never seen it. He sat on the couch, the container of chicken on his lap. I sat on the floor at his feet, picking at my food. As Bill Murray's clock radio flipped to 6:00 a.m., Sonny and Cher blurted out the first lines of "I Got You Babe." I wasn't really paying attention to the movie, and I doubted he was either. None of it seemed particularly funny that night. My heart was aching, my mind reeling, as I tried to fathom what it was like for him. How does one process that the immediate future holds only decline and then death? And not just death, not just sudden non-existence, but a slow death that promises to methodically wall its conscious victim within a lifeless body like Edgar Allan Poe's character Fortunato in *The Cask of Amontillado*—a man shackled alive behind a brick wall, being constructed by a vengeful "friend." A wall that would gradually conceal him in silence, confine him to a hidden and anguishing end.

To be given news like Woody was given must slash

at the healthy brain like a rogue machete. And yet, every day, every hour, someone is given similar news. Someone is told they will lose their ability to see, or they will soon not remember the people they love, and someone else wakes in a hospital bed to be told that an accident has changed everything. It is information that dwarfs the day-to-day concerns of life a week earlier.

Bill Murray's clock radio flipped to 6:00 a.m. Sonny and Cher started singing. Again.

This was early April and, while it was not clear if my mother would recover, the thought of her being discharged—while my dad would need so much care and attention—presented a host of possible scenarios, none of them very appealing. She was unaware of Woody's prognosis, which was a blessing. What concerned me though was, *should* she recover, she *couldn't* care for him—especially if he lived long enough to lose his ability to walk or use his hands. And the thought of someone else stepping in to help him (*me*) could very likely trigger her darker instincts.

Even in health, my mother was hard-pressed to care for herself. Not for any clinical reasons, but because she had always relied on him. For everything. To the point she would no longer *attempt* to open a child-proofed bottle. She would just hand it to him.

Though the term "enabler" was not around—or was at least esoteric—when they began their relationship, Woody was a textbook example. I suppose part of the reason was that he enjoyed solving problems, working on things, figuring things out. In my youth, I remember he was always over at the neighbor's house helping them build a fence or a garage. He was forever working under the hood of our car or someone else's. Nor had I ever seen him drive past a stranded motorist. He was always jumping in, fixing someone else's problem.

But this inclination to do things for her reached an absurd and, okay, alarming level: A few weeks after her death, when we were going though things in their garage, I uncovered a wheelchair beneath a pile of blankets. "A wheelchair? How come you have a wheelchair?" I asked.

His speech was difficult to understand, but I was able to get the gist of it. It was for my mother.

"Mom needed a wheelchair? When was that?"

"When we went to Vegas."

I looked at him.

He shrugged, "She got tired of walking between casinos."

I stood for a moment, processing it, looking at him with incredulity. "Seriously?"

He shrugged again like *Whata ya gonna do?*

When *Groundhog Day* was over, I told Woody he could sleep downstairs in Cath's and my bed, since she and the boys were gone. It was probably more comfortable than the bed in the loft. And the loft was somewhat of a pain in the ass to get up to, and down from, with a steep and treacherous stairway that left little room for slips or missteps. I'd stay in Joe and Henry's room.

I took him downstairs so he could get ready for bed. When, a few moments later, he pulled back the bed's red jersey sheets, I went into the bathroom, brushed my teeth and returned. He was curled up on my side of the bed, facing his own image in the darkened window.

It was a moonless night and even the stairway outside the window had disappeared behind his reflection. For the first time, he looked small. I walked to his side of the bed, leaned down and touched his arm. He looked up at me. I told him to sleep well. He patted my hand and smiled slightly. I turned out the light and closed the door behind me.

In the boys' room, I lifted the Mickey Mouse sheets of Joe's bed and squeezed myself in, jamming my feet in at the end of it. I stared up at the glow-in-the-dark moon and stars plastered on the ceiling and walls—annoying plastic things that would have to eventually be torn down, no doubt taking paint and drywall with them. Beside Henry's bed, there were magazine pages with pictures of elephants taped to the wall. At five, elephants—pronounced "el-phants"—was a subject he could talk about *indefinitely* and somewhat knowledgeably, while following me from room to room to room. To room. Once, in fact, his pachyderm lecture continued until I walked into the bathroom and closed the door in his face. There he waited patiently until I reemerged and picked up where he left off.

Above me, on Joe's side of the room, Joe had taped a full-page ad of a Dodge Ram pickup. I had no idea why. He was not a kid enamored with trucks or cars or Dodges or even rams—just Power Rangers and, believe it or not, chickens—so the taped ad was a little baffling.

I was relieved to be alone after a long day. Relieved to escape the gaze of my dad's eyes as they betrayed the fear in his heart. I was exhausted from caring so much about a man who asked for nothing. Expected nothing. And then I thought about him lying in the other room, in my bed, and I thought maybe I should get up, go in there, crawl into bed with him. I thought about it, almost got out of bed and then I closed my eyes and fell asleep.

Forever since, I regret having not done so.

In the time that transpired between his original diagnosis and our return to UCLA, Woody went back to his empty house in Pahrump. A few days after he got home, my mother died. My brother and I flew out to help with the arrangements and the multitude of other things that needed tending to. *Becker* was still on hiatus, and would be until early June. My boss, Dave Hackel, heard about my mother's death and sent flowers to the house in Pahrump.

A week and change later, Woody flew back to L.A. for his next appointment at UCLA (to take Dr. Graves up on his offer to enroll him in the Creatine Program). As we stood at the front desk of the Neurological Center, I let the receptionist know that Claude Woody was there for his appointment. The receptionist, a heavyset woman in her twenties, checked the appointment book and seemed a little confused.

"What was the last name again?"

"Woody. W-o-o-d-y. Like the woodpecker. First name, Claude." (I have included this woodpecker thing since college—perhaps to deflect from the pornographic implications the name might conjure up.)

"Woody…" She flipped a page back and forth. "And you made an appointment?"

"Yes." I waited to let her search the book further, adding, "That's why we're here. Because of the appointment we made." A hint of sarcasm was seeping out.

"And who was the appointment with?"

"Dr. Graves."

"Dr. Graves?"

"Dr. Graves, yes. That's my dad's doctor. So we figured that's who we would make the appointment with." The sarcasm a little less veiled.

She looked confused, then more confused. Then she got up and moved off to confer quietly with another receptionist. My dad and I exchanged a look. When she returned, she sat and said, "Well, I don't know who made the appointment, but Dr. Graves is on vacation."

Now *I* was confused. "He's on...vacation?"

She looked to the other receptionist, who nodded. She looked back at Woody and me. "Yes."

"But...Dr. Graves was the one who told us to make the appointment. For the Creatine Program."

The other receptionist stepped over to us. "Dr. Graves will be back the second week in May. You'll have to reschedule for then." She was an older woman, abrupt, well-hardened to the likes of troublemakers like my father and me.

"Well, see, my dad flew out here from Nevada for this appointment. Is there someone else who can...help us? With the Creatine Program?"

She shook her head. "I'm sorry. Dr. Graves runs the study. He needs to be here. You'll have to make another appointment."

I stood there for a moment just, well...blinking. And then I thought to posit that, if the study involved, say, record-keeping and just the dispensation of Creatine powder, "maybe somebody *else* could do that *for* Dr. Graves." It seemed reasonable to me that nearly any mildly intelligent UCLA employee might be capable of scooping out powder and then writing something down. Admittedly, as I presented this idea, my growing sarcasm had given way to something deeper, more acidic, and it hit the nurse's stone face like a pebble does a national monument.

So...we made another appointment. And this time, I was sure to ask if the doctor would be in town when the appointment would take place. The receptionist didn't appreciate my question, but I was pissed off... *and*, okay, I might've been showing off a little for my dad.

So Woody flew back to Pahrump, and then returned again a couple of weeks later. We drove over the hill, back to UCLA. This time, Dr. Graves was there. He was pleasant enough—and why not, he'd just gotten back from vacation. But now, in the exam room, as he looked over his clipboard, *he* was a little confused. "So, you're here...why?" he asked.

"Oh," I said, "we wanted to take part in the Creatine program. The one you mentioned when we were here in April."

"The Creatine program..." he said, drawing a deep breath and putting the paperwork aside to rub his neck, as though someone had just stuck a small knife into it. With some chagrin, he then let us know that *unfortunately* the university, well, someone *in* the university, *unfortunately*, didn't submit the, uh, necessary paperwork, *unfortunately*, in time to renew the, uh, study's license. *Unfortunately*. The Creatine study was no longer open to enrollment. He was quick to add, however, that they'd only missed the deadline by a mere three days—this, as though he was presenting us with a significant mitigating factor.

I turned and looked at my dad, maybe because I couldn't look at the doctor. I was awestruck by the level of professional what? Nincompoopery?

Before we left, and just to put some icing on what was turning out to be a giant piece of shit cake, I asked Dr. Graves what the difference was between the Creatine used in the study, and the Creatine *anybody* could pick up at the local health food store.

He shrugged. "Nothing."

I blinked again; I was becoming a cartoon character. *Blink, blink.* "Nothing?"

He shook his head. "Nope."

"But, I don't understand," I said, because I didn't understand.

"Oh, well see, the Creatine study was basically a double-blind test," he said.

"Ah..." I said, nodding like an attending physician. "So...my dad would have been taking a Creatine pill that may, or may not, have been filled with Creatine?"

"Exactly," he said.

"Why then..." I was trying not to be confrontational, "what would be the advantage of enrolling in the program—I mean, if it still existed—as opposed to, say, walking down to the corner GNC and picking up a bottle of Creatine with actual Creatine in it?"

"Well, there isn't really any advantage," Graves said. "But your participation in the study would help research."

An image flashed across my mind of two hands, mine, grasping the diminishing tufts of hair on either side of his head and bringing his face quickly down into my knee. And, okay, yes, I do appreciate the benefit of medical research studies—I just wasn't in the mood.

The ride back to Studio City was a long one. My father and I marveled that a place like UCLA could be home to such an extraordinary level of utter incompetence...though I might have used other words to express as much.

At least, we reasoned, we would not have to go back there again.

Ever.

Well, okay, we'd never have to go back there again *after* we went back there again and saw the speech pathologist, whom we had an appointment with a few days later.

The speech pathologist, we were happy to discover, was not on vacation. She was a middle-aged woman with sharp features and a schoolteacher's bearing. She seemed nice enough, as she explained to me everything she could help us with. I was encouraged. We were encouraged.

Then she turned to address my dad.

When she did, her demeanor changed dramatically: She talked slowly, purposefully, carefully, over enunciating each syllable like she was talking to a man who ate paste. She was suddenly a wealthy Texan in Europe, blasting out words as though their volume transcended all language barriers. At first, I thought she was kidding...which would have been an interesting and, well, brave comedic choice. But I soon realized, she wasn't.

This talking-to-the-mentally-challenged syndrome

was something I would see rather frequently around my dad. Admittedly, when he first started to lose his ability to talk, his speech went from slurred to garbled to pitiful guttural noises, so he *sounded* a little off. Most often though, those we interacted with—receptionists, phone installers, tellers, delivery people—would turn to me and talk about him in the third person. "Where does he want me to put the propane tank?" "Have your father sign here." "Would he like something to drink?" And, on those rare occasions when someone just sat down and talked to him like he was a person, I was convinced of their humanity *and* infinitely grateful.

But nobody had talked to him like this. Like...*this*. And she was a speech pathologist.

What made matters worse, she didn't even acknowledge any of the jokes my dad and I shared. After all, it was how we managed to skirt addressing directly some of the more horrific aspects of the disease that he was being assaulted by. It was a diversion, our jokes, but we needed that diversion. By this time, too, Woody had become pretty good at conveying to me sarcasm—or acknowledging that something inane had been said—with a look. In fact, he got good at what I called the Jack Benny response. That casual look Benny so famously gave in the presence of absurdity, a look that underscored his ethereal patience with a lesser of God's creatures.

When the speech pathologist began to explain to Woody which foods he would and wouldn't be able to eat in the months to come, her tone took on a pedantic, lecturing quality. She told him that he'd eventually have to mix this slimy stuff into his water, so that he'd be able to drink just water. Then she said, like it or not, he'd need to make a decision about having a feeding tube surgically inserted into his stomach—and she *strongly* recommended that he opt for it sooner than later, since it was inevitable. All of this said, of course, loudly and in a perfectly-enunciated staccato. (Still unsure how all this fell under the domain of "speech pathology," but there it was.)

I could see it was starting to get to my dad. How could it not? He shifted uncomfortably under her close proximity, and then glanced at me. I knew what he was trying to convey. After another moment, I put my hands on my knees and stood up. I thanked her and took my dad's arm to indicate that we were on our way out. She seemed a little surprised at our suddenly making for the door. But honestly, enough was enough. That's when she mentioned something about a machine that would talk for Woody.

Huh?

It was a small computer that he could type a word or a sentence into, push a button and have it say the word or words for him. It was called a LightWRITER.

And it was cool. It was perfect.

The speech pathologist said that Woody's insurance would cover the cost (about six thousand dollars), and that she would get the application started right away. We could expect to have a new LightWRITER within a couple of weeks.

Finally, UCLA was doing something *for* us, instead of *to* us. On the way to the car, I said, "Watch, Dad. It'll be part of a double-blind thing. The machine might work, might not." He laughed. But, good God, he *needed* this machine.

He had not yet moved to Los Angeles and was, by now, living alone in Pahrump, flying back and forth to L.A., sorting out medical bills, trying to sell his house and a car and a trailer; as well as dealing with all the things one must deal with when preparing to move—all without being able to talk. His neighbor, Henry Lingam, helped out to an extraordinary degree, and my aunt Oleta and I were out in Pahrump as frequently as we could be. But still, life had become a colossal pain in the ass for Woody.

Soon though, *soon* we would have the Light-WRITER.

In only a couple of weeks. A mere fortnight.

A month later, we had still not received it, nor had we heard from the speech pathologist at UCLA. After getting the run-around on the phone, I finally drove over to the university, where I lurked in the hallway near her office like a paparazzo. When I saw her, I (re)introduced myself and asked about the LightWRITER. She seemed flustered, said the insurance company was holding everything up, that they were being very persnickety about "buzz words" on the application. "They have to have all these very specific buzz words before they'll do anything. So, I'm working with them now." I asked then if there was anything I could do to expedite the situation because my dad was having a hell of a time trying to get through the things he had to get through, and that machine would sure come in handy. She said there wasn't anything I could do, that she was in the process of re-filing the application after including all of their required "buzz words."

After speaking with her for about twenty minutes,

what I began to realize was that the "buzz words" she was referring to had to do with Woody's voice. Though she wouldn't come out and say it, the problem was this: The application she'd sent in didn't mention *that he couldn't speak!* Now, I'm the last person on God's green earth to defend a medical insurance company—I liken them to the very cancers they prevent people from getting treatment for—but, in this instance, I saw their point. Yes, it would be important to know that my dad COULD NOT SPEAK! Again, I was flabbergasted by the ongoing nincompoopery. I was (sorry for this) speechless.

It was a month and a half before the LightWRITER was finally shipped. By then, hiatus was over and I was back to work in the *Becker* rewrite room. I joked to the other writers that "at least these people at UCLA aren't in charge of life and death situa—oh wait, hold on."

The experiences brought to mind for me how helpless my father would have been had he to navigate this Looking Glass quagmire by himself—without a (literal) voice, without leverage, without someone in his corner. More than the inconvenience it caused us, him, it made me feel for the many who were, are, alone and afflicted with terminal or life-threatening illnesses; the vulnerable who do not have a persistent son or a determined sister or neighbor to step in, to speak up for them, to hack through the jungle's foliage. My heart ached for the elderly with debilitating diseases that render them powerless in the jaws of an impossibly complex system. Or worse, those severed from the system altogether, dashed aside by the machinery's profit-driven cogwheels.

What do they do? Where do they go?

FOUR
Pahrump to Los Angeles

"Ah hell, Los Angeles is nothing but Goddamn smog and freeways," I remember my dad saying many times to friends or neighbors when I was a kid. "You couldn't get me to live down there for a million bucks."

So, when Woody and I made plans for him to live closer to us, Los Angeles was, of course, out of the question. I made appointments to look at houses in Woodland Hills, Ventura and even Ojai. Then, one day, as we got in the car to drive up to Ojai, I told him I had run across a house for sale in Studio City. Casually I mentioned that we could stop by, just stop by, on our way out of town, just have a quick look. That's all. "Then we get back in the car and drive to Ojai."

He agreed to it with thinly veiled skepticism. So a few blocks from our house, I took a quick right and turned onto Cantura Street. I slowed down a little to let him take in the wide and languid street beneath huge elm and poplars that arched overhead like the arms of children playing *London Bridge is Falling Down*. We cruised beside a shady sidewalk and deep green lawns, both shaggy and well-groomed, that flanked short driveways and skirted brick and stone walkways. Inviting front porches nestled beside cozy living room windows. It was a street that beckoned one to get out of the car and walk a dog, or push a baby in a stroller. The type of neighborhood that made you want to knock on a neighbor's door and ask to borrow a cup of cardamom or a Weed Eater. They were mostly two and three-bedroom homes, a hodgepodge of various styles, most of them built in the 1920s and '30s; a casual version of something Norman Rockwell might've come up with.

Though Woody was trying desperately to hang onto his skepticism, the veneer was cracking. The house for sale was near the end of the block, a couple of houses away from the one used for *Malcolm in the Middle* (dressed down during shooting with a dead lawn in front and weeds on the roof). There was a basketball hoop over the garage door and a couple of lazy willows on the lawn of the front yard. We walked through the three bedrooms, two bathrooms, the TV room, living room, the kitchen (with a Sub-Zero fridge), and then stepped out to a backyard with a lawn and plenty of room for Woody's dog Ace.

And...it was only a few blocks from our house.

He didn't say anything as we got back in the car and headed for Ojai—about an hour and a half from Studio City. We met there with a Realtor who was going to show us a few homes. After the first one, we got back in the car to drive to the next, and Woody took the little note pad from his pocket (we hadn't yet received the LightWRITER) and wrote, "I like Studio City."

I smiled. "Okay. Then let's do it." We drove back to the house on Cantura Street and I made an offer.

When Woody found out how much the house cost, he was dumbfounded (house prices in Los Angeles are not like those in Pahrump). He shook his head and indicated that it was too much. In one of those moments that a son dreams of, I told him not to worry about it—I was buying. I suppose it was an exaggerated form of the first time one sits at a bar with his dad, and snaps up the tab. "I'm getting this round, Dad."

My dad's sister Oleta had driven out to Studio City to help; to direct the movers, to unpack boxes, to organize the kitchen. She lived in Globe, Arizona (some 460 miles away), and though she was 75 at the time, she was forever willing to jump in her car and make the arduous drive back and forth between the two cities. She, like many of us, was thrilled with the idea of spending time with my dad.

For Woody, the move was like surfacing from the depths of the ocean to breathe fresh air and take in a bright blue sky. With his sister there to help put things away and get settled in, his son and his son's family a few blocks away, a street, a neighborhood, that was not only beautiful, but welcoming...it was a new world for him.

And...the LightWRITER had finally arrived!

He could now communicate with his new neighbors, open a bank account by himself, ask a question at the grocery store, and be specific when he needed something from the employees at the little Studio City Hardware store, his new favorite place to go. They were a bunch of regular guys who worked there, some with checkered pasts maybe or an early disdain for school that caught up with them in their late 20s, early 30s— not unlike a good many of the guys in the garages where

Woody had spent a big part of his life. He was particularly fond of two guys, Jim and Jackson, who could seriously tell you the difference between an anchor, a carriage and a flange bolt without batting an eye. Still, they were juvenile enough to smirk if someone asked for "black caulk." A few weeks after Woody had moved into his new house, I went with him to pick up some nails for something he was building. As we walked in, I heard, "Hey, Woody!" and, "There he is!" and, "How you doing, Woody?"

His first week in his new house, his neighbors, Tim and Kerri, invited us over for a barbecue. Kerri was studying nursing at the time, and made sure Woody had her phone number to use "anytime, day or night. Really. Seriously, Woody, just call. I'll know it's you." Tim, a sports writer for the *LA Times,* was over occasionally to check on my dad and to drag his two little boys, Timmy and Connor, back home after they had come to visit Woody or play with Henry and/or Joe.

Gordy, down the street, would often stop by while he was out walking his German shepherd. A stout, balding man with a warm smile, he was, I came to learn, something like the mayor of the street. If you were in your front yard when Gordy came by, he'd always stop and chat.

Michelle, next door—named by her parents after the Beatles' song—came by occasionally to retrieve her cat, who was unafraid of dogs and saw Woody's open front or back door as an invitation to come in and hang out, eat some dog food.

Of course, Cath and the boys were in and out all the time, as well as the boys' twenty-something nanny,

Claudia, who always made Woody laugh. She was a diminutive spitfire from El Salvador, and he was greatly entertained by her raw chutzpa (to borrow from Yiddish). On one occasion, she was on her way over to his house to pick up the boys, but was delayed by a police car in front of her on Ventura Boulevard that was (in her opinion) going too slowly—so she honked and gestured for them to get out of her way. Serious. Naturally, they pulled her over and, when they did, she explained that they were going too slowly and that she was in a hurry, so yes of course she honked. *Then* she wanted to know *why* they were going so slowly on a big busy street like Ventura Boulevard.

That she was not ticketed or charged with, oh, I don't know, a slew of possible offenses, trumped up or real, was probably due to a similar amusement on the part of the cops. When she explained all of this to us over at Woody's house, she of course did not find any of it humorous and was in fact still irritated that (a) the cops were going so slowly in the first place, and (b) they pulled her over and delayed her even further. Woody, on the other hand, was giggling throughout her explanation.

Shortly after settling into his new house, my dad went out and bought bunk beds for the middle bedroom. "The boys' room." Something both of them were very excited about.

After that, they spent most weekends over at Grampa's, where on Saturday mornings they woke to the wafting aroma of bacon frying and pancakes browning on the griddle. Neither had ever been an early riser, but on those mornings, there was never a problem getting them out of bed. They'd wander out in their pajamas to sit and yammer at Grampa about their various observations, while he filled their plates with hotcakes and sizzling bacon, then handed them the syrup (none of which he could any longer eat). Then they'd all move into the TV room and situate themselves on the floor and couch to watch *The Power Rangers, Scooby-Doo, SpongeBob SquarePants,* Henry and Joe slurping up pancakes and syrup-covered bacon, my father drinking his fruit smoothie—or later pumping liquid "food" into his feeding tube—all the while enduring the sweet smell of foods he loved, and worse, his grandsons' choice of entertainment.

Unlike the home I grew up in, and the one Woody had grown accustomed to, this one was filled with laughter and noise, music, jokes and many voices, young and old, real and synthetic. It was a comfortable and comforting environment, and it became clear to me that he wanted as much of it as he could get.

One morning, after I dropped by his house on my way to work, he walked me out to the curb, and then pressed the button on his LightWRITER: "HAVE A GOOD DAY." After I got in my car, and he walked back toward the house, I turned the ignition and checked a message on my phone. A moment later, I put the car in gear and was about to pull out when I glanced in the rearview mirror and saw that my dad had picked up a basketball that Henry or Joe had left on the lawn. I watched as he dribbled it a couple of times and took a shot at the hoop over his garage door. And as he retrieved it to take another shot, I smiled and drove off, feeling as though I had accomplished something significant.

FIVE

The Adoption

He was much taller in real life.

"Mr. Danson, you have a moment to sign something?"

"Sure."

I handed him a piece of yellow paper and a pen.

"Who's it to?"

"Laurie. My girlfriend. She's got a thing for you."

We were standing on the walkway of Lucy Park on the Paramount lot, between the *Cheers* and the *Taxi* soundstages. Lucy Park was a small, tree-lined grassy area—named after Lucille Ball—in front of the building that was used as Jefferson High School in *Happy Days*.

It was my first encounter with Ted Danson. *Cheers* was in its second or third season, and my girlfriend at the time, Laurie, was in love with him. I was a wiry production assistant on a sitcom called *Family Ties*. After he'd scrawled, "To Laurie. All the Best, Ted Danson," he handed me the paper and pen.

"What's your name?" he said.

"Russ," I said. "Listen, thanks. She'll really appreciate this."

He smiled again, said, "Take it easy, Russ," and moved off.

I had seen him "in person" only once before when I

was a production assistant on *Benson* (the *Soap* spinoff from the early '80s starring Robert Guillaume). Ted was a guest star on the show, playing Caroline McWilliams' love interest and eventually her husband. This was before he was famous, but I remember being struck by his ease. When he was acting, there was a casual way about him, a fluidity to his movement. He made it all look easy, the way an accomplished ice skater makes a triple axel look simple.

Although his success in Hollywood was not brought about by just luck, he has said many times how lucky he has been. In his career, in his life. And indeed, the kindness I have seen him show his co-workers bespeaks the sincerity of that gratitude. And what was reassuring for those of us who worked with him on *Becker* was that he'd already been at the top, so he was who he was. He wasn't going to suddenly turn into a crazy person with the onset of fame.

My working relationship with Ted began (somewhat disastrously) in the fall of 1998, at the beginning of *Becker*. He and wife, Mary Steenburgen, invited the writers, the other actors and their families over for a small Christmas party.

Their house rested on a slight incline at the end of a tree-lined driveway a couple of blocks off Sunset Boulevard in Brentwood. But it was not the sort of house you'd expect to see, given the type of stars they were. It was, in fact, relatively modest in that regard. A contemporary two-story with a kitchen off the living room, a TV room on the other side of the kitchen that led to a small brick patio in the back, a lawn and a pool. It was nice, I'm sure expensive, given its locale, but it wasn't over-the-top. In fact, it had a country-ish homey feel that made you want to take your shoes off and sit on the floor.

Catherine and I brought Henry and Joe along because Ted had made a point of saying that kids *especially* were welcome. The boys were four and two (respectively).

Cath, of course, was unruffled by any of the boys' shenanigans and, in true Aussie fashion, made it a point to enjoy the party. That she was so relaxed about the impact our children had on other people in, say, restaurants, grocery stores, airplanes, etc., is a quality that I have long envied and cursed. I was forever overly concerned about, plagued by, what others thought of the kids' behavior. The differences between Cath and me—in more than just parenting—is certainly prime fodder for a psychology class. Our background explains much of it. She was raised by parents in a stable relationship, along with three siblings near her age, in the midst of a nurturing and consistent neighborhood. I was raised in the midst of a volatile marriage, with a brother much older than I (gone before I was eight), then uprooted every couple of years to move to another town. Yin and yang, I suppose, like many successful—and for that matter, unsuccessful—marriages.

At one point during the party, I was looking for Henry, and stepped outside onto the back porch, where I found Ted, on his hands and knees, picking up pieces of glass and wiping up spilled wine, while Henry stood nearby looking on. Henry had apparently sailed through the area and knocked a glass of wine off the coffee table onto the brick patio. As Ted picked up another shard of glass and dropped it into a paper towel, he reassured Henry that it was no big deal, that accidents happen, not to worry about it. I apologized and helped Ted clean up, while he assured me as well that it wasn't a big deal.

A moment later, after Ted had gone back into the house with the broken glass and paper towels, I saw Joe walking in from the back lawn, clutching something in his hand. He was headed for the back door of the house.

"Hey, Joey?" I said, approaching him. "Whatcha got there?"

"I just found it," he said with some pride, opening his fist to show me a wad of dog shit. "It was just layin' out there on the grass."

I felt fortunate to have stopped him when I did. We returned the dog shit to the lawn, and then we went inside to wash up.

Figuring they were with their mom, I settled into one of the oversized chairs in the living room and began to relax near the fireplace. I was talking to a couple of the other writers, when I glanced over at the other side of the room and saw both Henry and Joe carefully examining one of Ted and Mary's cane chairs. It was an unusual chair in that the seat was deep and topped by a sheet of clear Plexiglas, so that one could look down into the seat and see a miniature room with tiny chairs, a small table, even a little piano. I figured they were staying out of trouble, so I loosened up and yacked with my co-workers. A few minutes later, I glanced over and saw that Henry had removed the Plexiglas to allow Joe access to the chair's inset diorama. Joe, I saw, was helping himself to a few of the miniature chairs. I flew out of my chair like it was a medieval catapult.

"Joe, Joey! No! Don't, don't do that! Here, here, give those to me. Give those to me," I said, carefully taking the tiny chairs from him. And, as I placed them gently back in the larger chair, Ted came around the corner from the kitchen, and saw what was going on. I told Henry to replace the Plexiglas and then told both boys to leave it alone, leave everything alone. Sit and leave everything alone. As I turned back to apologize to Ted, he was laughing. "I'm really sorry," I said, red faced. "I didn't know they could open it. Really, I'm sorry."

"Don't worry about it. They're industrious kids." He patted my shoulder and moved off again.

By the time my dad had moved to Studio City, the show was back in production for its third season. One of the first episodes we shot included a scene where John Becker (Ted) accidentally blows up a car. His character had stopped smoking but, desperate for a late night cigarette, he "borrows" a neighbor girl's bike to get himself to a small liquor store in New York City (where the show was set). When he finally gets his precious cigarettes and lights one up, he tosses the match aside, then gets back on the bike and wobbles off. The match ignites an oil stain on the pavement, a flame makes its way to an old beater parked in front of the liquor store and the car bursts into flames. Obviously it was a scene that couldn't be shot on the soundstage in front of an audience, since it involved, well, a car bursting into flames, so we shot the scene one evening on the back lot of Paramount.

I thought my dad might enjoy watching us film it,

so I mentioned it to him and Oleta, who was back in town again, staying with him. They, of course, were game, my dad especially because a car would be bursting into flames.

I arranged a drive-on for them and, at dusk, after the writers finished up in the offices, I walked over to the studio parking lot to meet them. It was the end of summer, the night air still warm, as we sauntered from there toward the New York street where the car was being prepared for the scene. Along the way, we passed another parking lot, backed by a huge wall—several stories high—painted blue with some scattered clouds. The wall was used for filming, and looked so real it wasn't uncommon to find a dead bird at its base, having flown into it. I suppose it was something of a dark compliment to the artists who created it. Or maybe a Darwinian test for birds?

As Woody and Oleta's tour guide, I explained that the parking area at the foot of the sky-scape was called "the tank," because it could be plugged up, filled with water and made to look like the open sea. It was an amazing spectacle to see. Especially when fog machines were added to pump a low-lying mist across the water's surface. And sometimes huge barrels on pistons were plunged into the water at the side of the tank to create traversing waves, while wind machines rippled the top of the water. Or, as when they were shooting *The Winds of War,* twenty-foot miniature battleships were set along underwater cables to make their way from one end of the tank to the other, pushed by unseen frogmen. So cool.

The brownstone walk-up section of the New York

streets was in shadows as we passed inviting stoops that fronted empty facades. We rounded a corner and came upon a much less impressive section of New York where the scene was going to take place—a back alley liquor store.

The crew had just started lighting the liquor store's front, so I took my dad and his sister over to a couple of the director's chairs amidst a row of them near the monitors. A few of the other writers were congregating there, doing nothing, kibitzing; so I made introductions and then gave Oleta and Woody their own headsets to listen in on the audio.

After the first take, Ted saw Woody and Oleta sitting with the writers, so he wandered over in his scruffy Dr. Becker overcoat and introduced himself.

"Oh, we know who you are," my aunt said. She, like Woody, was a big fan of *Cheers.*

My dad typed out, "HELLO, TED."

I explained that my dad had just gotten the LightWRITER, so we were still in the process of figuring it out, both him and me. Unfortunately, Woody's generation of men never learned to type, as there were no computers in his day, and typewriters were the domain of secretaries, who were nearly all women. *Mad Men* springs to mind. (Matt Weiner, btw, the creator of *Mad Men,* was one of the writers on *Becker* and sitting with us that night.)

After a moment, Ted was called back to the set, excused himself and went to work.

"He's so nice," Oleta said.

"Well, yeah," I said, having in the past regaled both her and my dad with stories of Cybill Shepherd, whom

I worked with a few years earlier. The *Cybill* experience, for me, was—as it has been for many people who've worked with her—uh, difficult. It was an experience that makes a writer, producer, director, actor or even a production assistant all the more grateful to work with someone like Ted.

After the director, Andy Ackerman, yelled cut and called for the next shot to be set up, Ted ambled over again and sat down with Woody and Oleta. After they talked for a bit, Ted asked more questions about the LightWRITER, so Woody showed him the basics, and offered to let him try it.

"Really?"

My dad nodded and handed it to him.

The actor put it on his lap like he was a kid with a new toy. He started to chuckle, while he typed out, "THE DIRECTOR IS AN ASSHOLE!" and pushed the button so that the synthetic voice would boom out in the direction of the crew. Andy didn't hear it, but someone near him did. They laughed and pointed Andy in our direction. As he walked over to have a look, Woody pushed the button again for Ted so that Andy could hear it. "THE DIRECTOR IS AN ASSHOLE!"

Now Andy wanted to type out something about Ted and, with Woody's help, did so. Andy's typed-out sentence was the intellectual equivalent of Ted's. This was, by the way, a phenomenon I would see many times among *men* in particular. They—well, we—for some reason, seemed overly fond of typing out obscene sentences and then listening to the machine repeat them. This same tendency wasn't true for women, due to an inherent sense of, what?, maturity?

When Andy was called back to the set a moment later, Ted and Woody were cackling away again about something one of them had typed. As they did, I glanced over my dad's shoulder, and saw my aunt look at me and roll her eyes. It was something she would do often in the months to come when Woody would sit down with a friend or two, new or old, and type out a dirty limerick or exchange obscene (often well-worn) insults—like the one about the horse someone rode in on. All of it, Oleta bore with a good deal of tolerance, patience and, yes, humor.

Though the liquor store scene on television was perhaps three minutes, the shooting of it took several hours. At one point, I had to run back to the production offices on the other side of the Paramount lot. When I returned I saw that Ted was on another break and again sitting with my dad and his sister. The hoopla of the dirty words had worn off and Ted appeared to be typing something more serious for Woody to read. I caught a glimpse of what it was from the scrolling LED display on the front of the machine. The first words that appeared were, "YOUR SON IS..." Immediately I felt uncomfortable and turned, pretending to look for my script, hoping to avoid that excruciating moment when someone felt inclined to compliment me to my dad. Whether sincere or from a sense of obligation, it was forever embarrassing. (Don't get me wrong, I enjoy getting a compliment, I'd just rather not be around when it happens.) A moment later I heard the machine blurt out, "YOUR SON IS A GIGANTIC SHITHEAD."

I turned back to them—my dad now chortling away—and put forth my best scornful look. "Wow," I said, "that is pretty cold."

Oleta started to laugh.

The *Becker* soundstage was #31 on the northernmost side of the Paramount lot. A few yards north of the stage was the Hollywood Forever Cemetery where Jayne Mansfield, Mel Blanc, Rudolph Valentino, Cecil B. DeMille—among many others, famous and not so—were resting (presumably) peacefully. From the stage, it was a good hike through Paramount to the parking lot, the "tank," and a bigger hike to our cramped and unimpressive production offices on the southwest corner of the lot.

The summer months on a television show—for the writing staff—are spent planning, writing and stockpiling scripts. That pre-production period, for many writers, myself included, is the most enjoyable part of the season because it is only about writing. There are no shows to produce, no run-throughs to go to, very few network/studio meetings, no late-night rewrites. Just planning and writing scripts on a relatively relaxed schedule. With all that was going on with Woody in his new house and the many problems he was facing, the timing was a blessing.

Of course, with the onslaught of production in the fall, all of that went out the window. *Becker* was a "multi-camera" show—meaning each episode was filmed in front of a studio audience, where several cameras rolled at once (with the exception, of course, of scenes like the one shot on the back lot). Filmings were scheduled for Tuesday nights, and Woody was determined to attend. It was not something I expected him to do, nor did I particularly want him to. I'd always felt something of an emotional burden when guests of mine arrived as part of the audience, since often they were stuck there for several mind-numbing hours, forced to watch take after take of the same scenes. But he wanted to be there, and frankly a side of me enjoyed having my dad show up in my workaday world.

After the first few weeks, he was given his own seat in the front row of the audience, just behind the rolling bank of monitors where we writers usually congregated. As the weeks turned to months, Woody not only began to feel like a part of the show, he actually *was* a part of the show. In one episode he was an extra, a patient waiting in Dr. Becker's office and then later he became the subject matter of an episode. During a week when publicity stills of my dad and Ted were being shot and a couple of news crews were on the set for the episode, the show's Executive Producer, Dave Hackel, laughed, turned to me and said, "Woody's now the show's fucking mascot."

What was amazing to me during that time was what transpired not just between Woody and Ted, but between my dad and the rest of the cast and crew. As my co-workers got used to seeing him around—and they became more comfortable conversing with him and his LightWRITER—I became aware of how much they were willing to extend themselves in ways I'd never expected. When the first of the season's episodes was about to air, Paramount paid for a *Becker* party at one of the nicer restaurants in the valley—Pinot Bistro—where white tablecloths flanked etched glass, and mahogany boxes framed rows of pricey wine bottles. I thought my dad might want to go, and indeed he did, so Catherine and

I took him along. One of the things I was growing to appreciate was his willingness to jump in, to show up, to be a part of social situations. He refused to hide. For understandable reasons, many afflicted with ALS choose to avoid social events, especially occasions that involve meeting new people. Frankly, I don't know if I could do what he did. But Woody wasn't afraid to step out in the open, to be seen as he was. And from this openness I began to see telltale patterns in the people who chose to interact with him. Those who were not intimidated by his inability to speak or his declining physicality were, by and large, accustomed to encountering life's realities and the vicissitudes of the human condition with its many and varied forms. And most important, they were, without exception, kind.

When I went off to get a drink, and Cath struck up a conversation with someone else, I was a little worried about him sitting by himself at one of the tables along the wall. I tried to be quick, hoping my abandonment would only be momentary. My worries were baseless however as I returned to find an attractive young woman named Caroline sitting with him while he showed her how the LightWRITER worked. When I saw her giggling at something, and Woody's broad smile, I was vaguely reminded of coming across a necktie on the doorknob of a college dorm room. She was bubbly and curious and talked a mile a minute, and it looked like my dad was getting along just fine without me.

I stepped away to chat with someone else, and turned back a few moments later to see that a young man was sitting with him. He and I didn't know each other well, since he worked only occasionally as an extra on the show. He was a guest of a friend of mine in Casting. Trent was in his mid-twenties, handsome with roguish, ruffled hair that jutted in several directions. He had a square jaw, stubble, and piercing dark eyes that gained depth when he squinted. He was a remarkable young man who was recklessly convinced he could learn things from an old guy like Woody. As well, he and Woody seemed to share a similar sense of humor and, in some ways, I'm sure my dad saw in Trent many of his own younger predilections. From their first encounter at Pinot Bistro that evening, their friendship would continue through the remaining months of my father's life. Like most of us in the early stages of a show business career, Trent was frequently "between jobs." In that downtime, he'd often pick up a movie at Blockbuster—anything John Wayne, Woody's favorite, or a host of other Westerns—and take it over to Woody's house, where the two of them would spend the afternoon watching it. Later, as things became more difficult for Woody to do, Trent would be over at the house rewiring a porch light, repairing the hot water heater or repairing a shelf in the living room.

On one occasion, when my aunt was there and working in the adjoining kitchen, Woody was sharing with Trent and me an email link he'd gotten from one of his two best friends (Elmer Hornoff or Noel Flecklin: he knew them from his days at PG&E and, yes, those are their real names). He had only just gotten his first computer with the move to Studio City, and his appreciation for the Internet centered largely on the receiving and relaying of dirty jokes from these guys. In this case, it was a picture of a busty woman in a diaphanous wife-beater, who lifted her shirt whenever the curser was moved across it. "Holy crap, Woody!" Trent bellowed. "That's fucking incredible!" I was laughing, while Trent howled and begged Woody to let him work the mouse.

Finally, my aunt had had enough. "Oh, for God's sake," she said, dropping a dishtowel beside the sink. "The three of you are acting like children!" She shook her head and walked out of the kitchen, while we exchanged guilty looks. And then turned back to pick up where we'd left off.

Along the back wall of Stage 31, behind the set that was Dr. Becker's office, a long industrial table offered up an abundant host of healthy and not-so-healthy snacks for the cast and crew. Beside it was a door that lead to a small room, lined with pots and pans, cans of food, cakes, pies, candy bars, bags of marshmallows and chips of every variety. This was Craft Services. It was run by Billy Nuzzo, a robust and sturdy Italian with a winning smile and the temperament of a honey badger.

Often, when one passed the open door to Crafts Services, they'd hear Billy's explosive bursts of outrage on the phone over any of a number of supply shortages: "Listen to me, you cocksucker! I need those chicken breasts by three o'clock, latest!" "Are you fucking kidding me? I've got sixteen cases of meatballs and no fucking sauce!" "Either you shitheads get the Tiramisu over here, or you can take the rest of the fucking order and shove it up your ass!" Most of us were used to hearing these diatribes and, if we were trying to have our own conversation outside Crafts Services, we would simply reach over and pull the door closed or move to a more pacific locale. Occasionally an unwarned and unprepared guest would find themselves beside Billy's door and well within earshot of his telephone threats. You could always identify such a person by their wide eyes.

At the end of a late filming one Tuesday night, Woody was backstage waiting for me, before we left. He ended up standing next to the Crafts Services table just outside Billy's door. The table was stacked with large half-eaten pizzas in boxes for the crew, which was standard when shooting went late, as it often did. As I made my way back there, Woody was being confronted by one of the more bumptious of the extras—officially they are called "atmosphere." She was a diminutive Asian woman, who had, on previous occasions, sidled up to me and said things that were baffling. When I came backstage to find Woody, I saw that he was being grilled by this woman. "Why don't you try the pizza? It's good. Go ahead, you try the pizza!" He was no doubt stymied by just how exactly to explain to her that it wasn't his *choice* not to eat the pizza. And how do you explain the symptoms of Bulbar syndrome ALS on a LightWRITER? "You think you gotta lose weight? You don't gotta lose weight! You skinny! Why don't you eat?"

Though she meant well, I was a little peeved that this woman took it upon herself to pursue the issue so relentlessly. I explained to her that my dad could no longer *physically* eat solid food, and thanked her (sarcastically) for her concern.

In the meantime, Billy had come out of his room to overhear some of it. When he learned that Woody couldn't eat solid foods and could only consume smoothies, he told us to hang on, hold on, stay right there, and went back into Crafts Services. A moment later, he reemerged with his arms around brimming plastic bags of fruit that had been chopped up earlier in the day. And for many of the Tuesdays that followed, Billy would insist Woody and I stop at Crafts Services before leaving, so he could load us up with huge plastic bags of fresh and frozen fruit. Sometimes more than we could fit in a freezer. It became our ritual. Until later, when I had to tell Billy that we couldn't take the fruit anymore because my dad could no longer swallow even smoothies.

For a time, while Woody could still eat some chewy foods, one of the show's production assistants, Kim, would cook up moist brownies and soft oatmeal cookies, and leave them on his front porch each morning with a small carton of milk. It was a sweet gesture that unfortunately was short-lived with Woody's dwindling ability to use the muscles of his throat.

After he gave up liquefied foods, he knew he could no longer avoid the surgery required for a gastrointestinal tube—the "G-tube." With it, he would have to pump liquid food directly into his stomach through a small tube that poked out just below his chest. It was an idea he hated and resisted for as long as possible, in part, because of the speech pathologist at UCLA—the one who talked to him like he was brain dead. She had *insisted* he get the operation done shortly after our meeting, thus engendering his defiant side. It was his way of saying fuck you to this woman, even though we hadn't seen her in months and she probably would have no idea who we were. But still. And though this wasn't the most rational of healthcare stratagems, I understood it. By the way, this defiant streak, this stubborn hold in the face of self-destruction, is a trait firmly inherited by Woody's grandson Henry. (Feel free to scan ahead for the "Cheerios on the kitchen floor" incident.)

Frequently, towards the end of an evening of filming, after the audience had filed out, I'd look over at the seats and see Saverio Guerra sitting next to my dad. Saverio played "Bob" on the show, the fast-talking, slicked back schemer. He felt a special affinity for my dad since his own grandfather died of ALS only a few years earlier. He knew all too well what Woody was facing and often commented on the courage it took to do so. Beyond that, he showed Woody genuine affection, and always sought him out for a hug and a hello. As did his wife Kim who, like Woody, was from Texas. Upon her return from a visit to her hometown, she was excited to show him photos of her favorite haunts. Then she reached into a bag and took out a sweatshirt with "Texas" scrawled across the chest. She handed it to Woody and kissed him on the cheek.

There were many small moments like that. Moments that sometimes I would only see from afar. Small acts of kindness, like with Tom in Set Decoration, who always yelled across the stage "Hey, Woody!" whenever my dad arrived. And Dick Kirshner, the easy-going avuncular guy from the network, who occasionally showed up with a hat or a t-shirt from one of the other CBS shows to give to Woody. Then there was Sharon in Wardrobe who saw that Woody was uncomfortable with the neck brace he eventually had to wear to hold his head up. It attached in the back and propped his chin up over a white padded armature. But it didn't fit right and he was miserable. She insisted he give it to her, took it to the back where she sewed in a new clip. She returned a few moments later and helped him put it back on. After a quick adjustment, it fit perfectly. He smiled and gave her a grateful thumbs-up. She hugged him.

Hattie Winston, who played "Margaret," Dr. Becker's no-nonsense nurse, always welcomed Woody with open arms and a loving/bordering-on-smothering hug. In fact, when she enveloped him into her ample bosom, he all but disappeared. At times, it left Woody looking a little dazed after an encounter with "The Girls," as Hattie called them. It soon became their not-so-private joke, something she considered her, uh, small gift to him.

Whenever Norm entered the *Cheers* bar, he was met with the familiar chorus of, "Norm!" To which he always had a clever quip in response.

George Wendt was not quite that guy, but almost.

He was doing a guest shot on *Becker* for his friend Ted. On show night I approached him to see if he'd mind saying hi to my dad. Wendt said sure, and, as we crossed the stage toward where Woody was sitting, I started to explain to him that my dad had been a big fan of *Cheers*, but couldn't exactly talk, that he had ALS and it had affected—

"Oh, I know about your dad," he said.

"Huh?"

"Yeah, Ted told me the whole story," he said, as we approached my dad. "He said your dad's a great guy."

Later in the evening, I'd heard that Wendt wasn't going to stick around until the end of the show. He was in a hurry to get home. I got the feeling he didn't like all the hobnobbing that sometimes took place at the end of a show night. From our brief interaction, I couldn't help but think he was fairly shy.

After he finished his scenes and changed back into his street clothes, I saw him wend his way over to Ted to say thanks and good-bye. I thought then he would slip out the back door and be gone. But he stopped at the side of the stage to scan the seats and the sets. A moment later he saw Woody, and then made his way from one side of the stage to the other, through all sorts of people who wanted to say hi, to pat him on the back and thank him for being on the show. My dad turned and saw "Norm's" broad smile as Wendt came up to him, said what an honor it had been to meet him and hugged him. Woody was flabbergasted. He pulled his Light-WRITER from his side and typed, "THANK YOU," then put his hand to his heart to say as much again.

Wendt smiled warmly at him, slipped out the door and was gone.

To tell you the truth, I was terrified.

Brian Fong, the show's Second Assistant Director, asked me one day if my dad wanted to do some "atmosphere work." "Atmosphere" are the unnamed people in the background who inhabit the set. They eat in restaurants, wait for trains, walk on sidewalks, etc. Brian thought it might be fun for Woody to do, since he'd been coming to the show every week, and since most everyone around there knew him. At the time, I agreed it might be fun, if he was up for doing it. That night, when I stopped by his house after work, I told him about Brian's idea. He thought about it for a moment and typed, "SURE."

The following Tuesday, he had to be at the *Becker* set around 5 p.m. to get instructions before filming. The audience was "loaded" by six (meaning "seated," in case you're thinking alcohol and/or drugs). The cast was usually introduced around 6:30, and then filming began. During the time before filming, the writers were usually either doing last minute rewrites or eating dinner, so I wouldn't be able to join Woody until the show started.

When I got to the set, I learned from Brian that he would be in one of the first office scenes. He was going to be a patient, waiting to see Dr. Becker.

A half hour later, the scene Woody was in was about to start, so Clare, the Third Assistant Director, told Woody to take his seat near the door in Becker's waiting room. He did, and then someone stepped up to take the LightWRITER away, since it wasn't necessary for the scene.

And then, there he was. Sitting in Becker's office. He looked through the magazines on the table in front of him and picked one up to read, the way a patient does. That was good. That would be good when the scene started. Except, that's when it occurred to me—what if he fucks up? I know it sounds easy to sit there like a patient, leafing through a magazine, but atmosphere have to make the same moves at the same time for each of the takes, or else the shots won't match. It can be a big problem. And Woody had never done this before. There were four cameras rolling at once, picking up every move—what if he looked up at one of them? An otherwise natural thing to do, but a move that ruins the shot. Something an inexperienced performer might do. Or what if he watched Ted enter and cross the room? What if he laughed at a line? Good God, there were so many ways to fuck up a take. Suddenly, I was a stage mother, horrified that the director would have to yell, "CUT!" Then someone would have to go in and tell Woody not to look at the camera; or what if, in the confusion, Woody forgot to pick up the magazine that he was supposed to be reading, and the director had to yell, "CUT!" and someone had to point out to my dad that he forgot to pick up the magazine and he ruined the shot? Or what if he sneezed? "CUT!" As I stood with several of the other writers over by the monitors, I was playing out a thousand awful scenarios, wishing he hadn't decided to do this and nearly pissing my pants.

Fortunately, Andy Ackerman was the director again. (Frequently in sitcoms there are a variety of directors throughout the season, though Andy directed most of ours.) He is a perennially nice guy, easy going, unpretentious, never panicked or out of sorts; he has the overall pacing and demeanor of a Dead Head, without (I'm assuming) the substance abuse. So if Woody fucked up, at least Andy wasn't going to get nasty about it.

After everyone was in place and the cameras were up to speed, Andy yelled, "Action!" The front door to the waiting room banged open and Dr. Becker entered, complaining about something as he crossed to Margaret at the front desk. My dad kept reading his magazine, so that was good. In fact, he actually looked like a patient leafing through a magazine.

So far so good.

Then, after Dr. Becker exchanged a few lines with Margaret, Woody put the magazine down...and got up to find himself another magazine! Oh my God, I thought, does he think he can just switch magazines? When he'd found another magazine, he crossed casually back to his seat, sat down and started leafing through it.

Andy yelled, "Cut!"

Shit.

Clare crossed into the set, headed for my dad. This was killing me. But then...she walked past him, picked up the magazine he'd gotten from the table and put it back where it had been at the beginning of the scene. Meanwhile, Woody had picked up the original magazine, opened it and appeared to be waiting for the next take. It was dawning on me that he hadn't fucked up. That he had actually been given some "business" to do and he'd executed it perfectly.

When all was in place again, Andy yelled, "Action!" Dr. Becker entered through the front door, crossed to Margaret, they exchanged a few lines, my dad put his magazine down, stood up, and crossed to get the other magazine. Then, as he started back to his seat...Ted fucked up.

"Cut!"

My dad put the second magazine back where it was, and crossed back to his seat. Ted went back out the door and a moment later Andy yelled, "Action!" Woody started casually leafing through the original magazine. And as Ted and Hattie exchanged lines, Woody put the magazine down and crossed to get the other one, *exactly* the way he had twice before!

He was perfect. He nailed it. I *knew* he would.

If you see the episode, his teeny bit will go by in a

flash. But I was as proud as any stage mother could be.

In the early spring, as the season was winding down, one Tuesday night Cheryl Downy appeared at my side on the stage. She was one of the co-producers on the show and in charge of a few hundred aspects of production. A small woman, thin, Cheryl had the demeanor of a coffee-swilling humming bird.

The show was starting soon and, when I heard her voice, I realized she'd come up beside me. "Your dad's not here yet."

"Oh," I said and looked over at his seat in the front row. "Well, he'll be here."

"You think he's okay?" she said.

"Huh, yeah. I saw him this morning. He's okay."

"Maybe he's having trouble getting here from the parking lot. Maybe we should send a P.A. to check?"

"I'll go out and check in a little while."

"No, I'll send a P.A."

And she was gone.

A moment later, he appeared, but it was obvious that he was fatigued from the walk. Cheryl appeared at my side again, this time with a series of questions. I acknowledged that, yes, he was tired from his walk to the stage. So I assured her that, after the show, I'd get a golf cart and take him back to his car. Then I promised her that the following week I would pick him up in the parking lot (the "tank") and bring him to the stage.

"Yeah," she said, clearly not convinced I was all that reliable. "No. No, I'll take care of this." I was about to defend myself, to tell her I *was* reliable but, as quickly as she'd appeared, she was gone again.

On the day before the next filming, Cheryl handed

me a slip of paper to give to my dad. "What's this?" I asked.

"Instructions for your dad. For tomorrow night. Make sure he gets that." She nodded at the paper and then explained what was on it. From that Tuesday forward: Woody was to drive onto the Paramount lot from the "Gower Street gate," the entrance *next* to Stage 31, not the front gate. I found out later that only two other people were allowed to use the Gower gate at that time of day: Kelsey Grammer (*Fraiser* was in production too) and Ted Danson. After Woody arrived, the guards at the gate would then notify Stage 31 to let Cheryl know that he was on his way. Then Cheryl would dispatch a P.A., who would leave to meet Woody out in front of the stage, take his car keys and drive the car over to the parking lot. Meanwhile, yet another Paramount guard was to arrive at the front of the stage to escort Woody onto the stage and to his seat in the front row. The whole process was to be reversed whenever he was ready to leave. All of which, in the weeks that remained, went off without a hitch.

That night, when I went by my dad's house, I read to him the instructions from Cheryl. He smiled a little and nodded. I gave him a look and said, "It's like you're fucking Elvis?"

He laughed and gave me one of those *What're ya gonna do?* shrugs.

The cast and crew picture is an end-of-season ritual, forever treated like a pain in the ass by the cast and crew during its execution, always appreciated when the image is finally returned to one and all. It's like the high school yearbook just before summer vacation. Ted, Hattie,

Saverio, Terry Farrell (the actress who played Reggie, owner of the diner) and Shawnee Smith (who played Linda, the office receptionist) with her little girl Verve, had all piled onto the couch in Dr. Becker's living room. Dave Hackel was standing behind the actors, while a sea of people surrounded them and the couch, filling the living room set, some standing, others sitting, especially those on the carpet in front of the couch. They were the hundred-fifty or so people it took to produce *Becker*.

The cameraman was on a ladder facing the group, about to snap the picture when someone noticed I wasn't there. I can't recall exactly what it was I was doing, but I heard someone shout for me to get my butt over to the living room set for the picture.

As I approached, another voice boomed out, "Where's Woody?" Then from someone else; "Yeah. Where's Woody?" I was standing in front of them now, looking for a place to sit. I shrugged and said I thought he was over in Becker's office. Another voice brusquely cracked, "Well, go get him!" Then another, "Yeah, get him!" "Get Woody!"

I crossed over to Becker's office where my dad and Oleta were waiting for me before they left for the evening.

"Hey, Dad," I said, "they want you over there for the picture."

He gave me a quizzical look.

I shrugged. "They want you in the picture."

"Well, go on, Claude," my aunt said. "Get over there. They're waiting."

I took my dad's arm and helped him out of Becker's chair. We crossed the stage together, toward the gathered group. As we did, I was thinking about where he might sit—the whole set was pretty crowded. But as we approached, Ted and Hattie moved apart from each other on the couch, while those sitting on the floor in front of them began to part, making an open pathway like a parted sea that led up to the couch. And like Moses, Woody walked through it to Ted and Hattie, where Ted stood up, took his arm and sat him down between himself and Hattie...in the middle of the couch (in the middle of the picture). Hattie hugged him. Ted put an arm around him and, as the pathway on the floor closed up, Ted said, "Okay, let's take this sucker."

Except...I was still standing there at the front of the group. "Yeah, great," I said. "So where do I sit?"

One of the production assistants said, "Why don't you sit on the floor?"

And that was the picture.

SIX

Breaking the Story

"Becker adopts a kid to prove that he's not an asshole."

"What? He hates kids."

"Okay, a dog. He adopts a dog."

"Been done. Besides, dogs are a pain in the ass to work with."

"Hey, what if a dog adopts Becker?"

"How's a dog gonna fill out the paperwork?"

"No, the dog starts sleeping outside Becker's front door. Becker can't get rid of him."

"Why would a dog do that?"

"I don't know. The dog relates to him? An angry dog?"

"Maybe the dog just keeps shitting in front of Becker's door?"

"The dog shits in front of Becker's door?"

"How 'bout a horse?"

"A horse shits in front his door?"

"No, Becker buys part of a horse. A racehorse. Thinks he'll make some money."

"Yeah, but the horse is tired, old...like Becker."

"Let's get off the animal stuff, huh?"

The room is quiet another moment.

"Okay, there's a fire in the diner. And everyone assumes it's Becker's fault?"

"Yeah, and it was actually set by a dog."

"Shut the fuck up about dogs."

And so it goes. Hour after hour, day after day. There are a million avenues, streets and lanes to go down, most turning out to be cul-de-sacs. Breaking stories for a television show is mostly a tedious, frustrating and often a contentious process, especially in sitcoms because episodes are, for the most part, modular. That is, one episode's story doesn't connect to the next. So each is a free-for-all. Each must be started from scratch.

Most often, the writers' room on a show is small and cramped, dominated by a conference table that is too big for the room and surrounded by six or ten comedy writers, in varying stages of recline, thinking, laughing, gossiping, staring at the ceiling, pitching, doodling, tossing food in the air to catch in their mouths. In many cases it is a matter of patience, wading through a hundred mediocre, bad and downright ridiculous ideas until somehow someone stumbles across something that is, at first, brilliant, then problematic, then not-so-great, then, wait a minute, *What if we flip this for that?*, and then wham, a story begins to emerge. It is why "rewrite rooms" (for sitcoms) are cesspools of vulgar free thought, the First Amendment unleashed to spew all things inappropriate, scatological, offensive, profane, mundane, shocking, extreme, macabre. Phil Rosenthal says (in his book *You're Lucky You're Funny*), "It's very hard to convey to anyone outside the [rewrite room] that no one in that room sees the shit joke as the height of comedy—just the opposite—and the reason we laugh so hard is because of how 'wrong' it is."

In the midst of the "shit jokes" and the plethora of

horrifying things said, there is the hope of finding something meaningful, heroic, truthful, kind; something that, on some level, speaks to the heart. And all the while, playing to the god Funny. It isn't easy, but it explains why there is, in most sitcom re-write rooms, an unspoken rule that nearly *anything* can be said, anything can be proposed, so that all avenues and streets and lanes can be explored. If even to throw them out and start again.

When someone in the rewrite room asked me if my dad was coming to the show the following week, I said I thought he was. Then one of the writers, Matt, made a joke about Woody getting stuck out at the guards' gate, and not being allowed onto the lot because he didn't have the right I.D.—so he got abusive (on his LightWRITER) with the guard. "HOW WOULD YOU LIKE A FOOT UP YOUR FUCKING ASS!" We could all imitate the voice of his machine by then—we often imitated the actors when pitching out lines—and suddenly we were all laughing and sharing one vicious insult after the next in our best synthetic LightWRITER voices. It's probably safe to say that all of the writers thought my dad was a nice guy, and that's what made it so funny. This nice little old man with his machine, standing outside the studio gates threatening a guard with, "HOW 'BOUT I RIP YOUR FUCKING HEAD OFF AND SHIT IN YOUR SKULL?"

We didn't know it would lead to a story, but that's often how it works. Suddenly we were playing with the idea of an older man who uses his LightWRITER to abuse people. Becker would help a nice old man get the machine, and then, once he gets it, he uses it to unleash all of his pent up frustration and anger.

By the end of the day, we'd come up with the bare bones of a story that we thought would work, and that I would write. Dave was on board—always essential—but before we went any further, I wanted to run the idea past Woody. The story wasn't really about him, but it'd be hard to deny he was the inspiration. So I felt like I needed his blessing.

That evening, when I got to Woody's house, I mentioned that we had been tossing around the idea of doing an episode about "an old guy with ALS, who can't talk anymore...so Becker gets him a LightWRITER." Woody, always a quick study, recognized the similarities between the character and himself. Then I said, once the old man can express himself (with the LightWRITER), "he becomes an asshole."

Woody laughed and gave me the okay. We were on.

The following day, when we started breaking the story into specific beats, another concern crept up. "If we do this story," I said to Dave at lunch, "I don't think we should make it about some bullshit disease like bad laryngitis or something. I think it should be ALS. But I don't know if the network is gonna be okay with that."

Dave agreed and got on the phone with Dick Kirshner at the network. To my surprise, they were fine with the idea.

Not that I thought anything profound could be said in a sitcom. In fact, I loath sitcoms with "a message." But I do believe that real things can be portrayed honestly, even tragic things, and they can still be funny. The greatest example of this is the classic "Chuckles The

Clown" episode of *The Mary Tyler Moore Show*—where a clown, dressed like a peanut, is killed by an elephant, and Mary can't help laughing through his eulogy.

At *Becker,* like most sitcoms, the finished script was very much a communal effort. The story itself was worked out as a group, usually on a whiteboard (my "specialty," for want of a better word), then the "writer" of the episode would write and turn in an outline. After notes from the show runner, the staff and sometimes the network or studio—the writer would write the first draft of the script, get notes again and often write a second draft. At that point, the script became the property of the show runner and the writing staff—who would take it through a series of rewrites and punch-ups, both before and during production. It is an arduous process that often seems to fly in the face of the creative gene, difficult for all, but especially difficult for the newer, more idealistic writers as, most often, their work is changed significantly and, very often, it's hard to even say who wrote what.

Then there's the review that rips the writer a new one for part of an episode the writer had nothing to do with. On the other hand, friends often compliment the writer for a joke he/she didn't write. That one never fails, and it's awkward. You learn to just say thanks (too hard to explain the whole rewriting process). Of course a lot of the time, the actors get credit for all of it. I once added something to someone else's script where Becker gets charged for phone calls to "Chico, California" (my alma mater). Weeks after the episode aired, some Chico State kids came to a filming and gushed over Ted, thanking him for coming up with that Chico stuff. Ted had no idea what they were talking about, since he usually forgot about scripts as soon as they were shot. (He hardly remembers anything about episodes of *Cheers*. Swear to God.) The other side of the coin is when an actor gets blamed for the words. I'd taken a swipe in a script at conservative Republicans—it wasn't a good joke and it wasn't meant to stay in the script (a placeholder), but for some reason it did—and Ted ended up getting hateful *hateful* letters addressed to CBS.

That wasn't so bad.

I usually dreaded the week of production when one of my scripts was being filmed. It is a taxing five-day process that involves casting, multiple rewrites that are often grueling, rehearsals, run-throughs and sometimes recasting; all of it culminating in three hours of filming in front of a studio audience. But, in this case, after I wrote the initial drafts of the script, I was surprised by some pretty easy rewrites—both before and during the week of production—due perhaps to the sensitivity of the writing staff to what I was going through with my dad. (And, believe me, you'll not see the words "sensitivity" and "writing staff" appear again in the same sentence.)

Certainly Dave was mostly responsible for the end product. It took many others though like Ian Gurvitz, the show's other Executive Producer, who'd come into the offices some days and rattle off a string of expletives about the traffic, his diatribe nearly poetic in its vitriol and structure. Perfect dialogue for Becker. Matt Weiner—who went on to write for *The Sopranos*, and then created and wrote *Mad Men*—always had great ideas and a great many opinions. And there was Kate Angelo, who at the time, was a "baby writer." She is no longer that, and is perhaps one of the most talented writers I've ever read. Marsha Meyers, another talented "baby writer," was forever willing to roll up her sleeves and jump into the fray.

Though I'd be hard pressed to remember specific jokes in the script, there's a good chance many of them came from Mike Markowitz. Mike is one of those rare talents with a near-encyclopedic mind and an ability to induce laughter that can leave a person gasping for air. He and Bob Ellison together were a dangerous combination. Bob was something of a legend in show business circles, having written for *The Mary Tyler Moore Show, Cheers, The Odd Couple, The Dean Martin Show, The Steve Allen Show,* ad infinitum. A tall soft-spoken guy in his late sixties, Bob's dry and quick wit often left me not just laughing, but astounded. And there was David Isaacs—arguably one of the nicest guys in the business (though it seems like a silly thing to argue about). He and his partner Ken Levine wrote and produced *M*A*S*H* and *Cheers* and just about everything else that's ever been on television, ever. As I write this, David is teaching writing to some very fortunate young people at USC.

When word finally came through from Casting that Tom Poston was going to play the part of my dad, I was thrilled. Poston was mostly known for playing "George," the pasty-faced, deadpan handyman on *Newhart.* He would be perfect for the character. "Joe Willekie" (named Joe after my son, and Willekie after a Marine Corps buddy of my dad's) would obviously not have a line, but it was important to get an actor capable of conveying intent, thoughts, emotions with his eyes, his face—and that was Poston.

He didn't know it, but I'd met Tom Poston once before, some fifteen or so years earlier when I was a writer at MTM (Mary Tyler Moore's company). I had an office next to the *Newhart* stage at what is now CBS Radford in Studio City. My aunt Oleta had come to visit, along with her mom, my grandmother, Arabelle. After we talked for a while in my office, we stepped outside, and there was Tom Poston, taking a break, hanging around in his *Newhart* overalls. I introduced myself to him, then introduced him to my aunt and my grandmother. Poston was very nice and, after a few moments, asked my grandmother—who was 80—if she'd ever done any acting, because he was looking for someone to star in an adult film he was producing.

After I told Woody that Tom Poston had been cast to play Joe Willekie, I told him the story about Poston's encounter with Grandma and Oleta. Woody was amused and when he came by the stage a couple days later to watch some rehearsals, I took him over to meet Tom. They shook hands and Tom mentioned how much he appreciated being cast in the role, that he was looking forward to show night. Woody pulled out his LightWRITER and typed, "YOU HIT ON MY MOM."

Though re-writes throughout the week were relatively painless, there was one point where I became very uncomfortable. It was when Joe Willekie's daughter, Helen, returns to (John) Becker's office to complain about her father and how he'd been abusing people with the LightWRITER:

HELEN

I thought it'd be so great if
my father could finally talk.
But, since he's had that machine he's been rude, he's
been insulting, and he uses
it to curse at everyone, including me. And he tortures
our poor dog with that damn
doorbell button. Every time
Biscuit hears it, he goes
crazy and runs for the door.
And my father does it <u>all</u> <u>day</u>
<u>long</u>.

(There's a button on the LightWRITER that, when
pushed, makes a doorbell sound to get people's attention. Earlier in the episode, John gives the machine to
Joe, and shows him how to work the doorbell button.)

JOHN

If you're asking me to take
the machine away, I can't do
that.

HELEN

I'm embarrassed to admit
this, but I liked him better
when he couldn't talk. (BEAT)
Is all this anger part of the
disease?

JOHN

Wouldn't you be angry?

                    HELEN
        It's just that I know we
        don't have much time left to-
        gether, and I don't want it
        to be like this.
                    JOHN
        Well, I suppose I could talk
        to him.
                    HELEN
        That would be great. But I
        warn you, he can be very
        abrasive.
                    JOHN
        Oh, don't worry about it. I
        deal with people like that
        all day long.

Helen's speech about not having "much time left to-gether" came into question and got tossed around the room. At one point, a version of it became very straight-forward. Especially when Helen was referring to her father's imminent death. "...we don't have much time left together," became, "...he's going to die soon..."

And I hated it.

But in the sitcom writing business, it's considered bad form to complain about line changes during the week when it's your script on the chopping block. Every writer is naturally inclined to protect his/her words, but a writer who does it too often becomes a pain in the ass. (The production schedule is too tight, there isn't time to squabble over a writer's vanity.) So I let it pass, hoping it would evolve to something more personally palatable. Unfortunately, it didn't. When it looked like the line change was actually going into the script, I had to speak up. My problem, I explained, was that Woody was going to be sitting in the audience, and the thought of having him hear a speech about how the character is "going to die soon" was more than I could bear. I justified my stand by saying that often characters dealing with big issues like the death of a loved one, don't speak in direct terms. They find euphemisms. A loved one hasn't *died*...they've *passed*. No one wanted to press the issue and, fortunately, Dave agreed, or just felt sorry for me, so the line was changed back to the softer version.

The last scene is between Becker and Joe Willekie in a bar, where John catches up with him to talk about Willekie's abusive behavior:

```
                    SCENE K


INT. BAR - LATER
(Bartender, John, Joe)


AN AVERAGE NEIGHBORHOOD BAR. JOE IS
THERE, WAITING FOR JOHN. A BARTENDER PUTS
A DRINK IN FRONT OF HIM. JOE TASTES IT
AND GRIMACES, THEN HE TYPES ON HIS MA-
CHINE AND PUSHES THE BUTTON.


              JOE (MACHINE)
        "I SAID BOURBON, NOT CAT
        PEE."


THE BARTENDER EYEBALLS JOE AND TAKES THE
```

GLASS TO REMAKE THE DRINK. JOHN ENTERS
AND APPROACHES JOE.

                    JOHN
          Hey, Joe, your daughter told
          me I could find you here.

THE BARTENDER RETURNS WITH JOE'S DRINK
AND SETS IT DOWN.

                 BARTENDER
          Now, if you've got a problem
          with that one, you can kiss
          my —
                    JOHN
          Hey, hey! This is a... well,
          it's a bar. But still.

                 BARTENDER
          (TO JOHN) You want anything?

                    JOHN
          Yeah. I'd like a
          scotch/rocks, please.

THE BARTENDER MOVES OFF.

               JOHN (CONT'D)
          (AFTER A BEAT) You know, with
          ALS, you're not supposed to
          be drinking.

JOE TYPES AND PUSHES THE BUTTON.

> JOE (MACHINE)
> "BECAUSE IT'S BAD FOR MY
> HEALTH?"

JOE TAKES ANOTHER DRINK. JOHN WATCHES
HIM, THEN...

> JOHN
> Hey, look, Joe, Helen wants
> me to talk to you. (A BEAT) I
> know it's bad. I know you
> didn't plan your life this
> way. You have a horribly un-
> fair disease.

JOE TYPES, PUSHES THE BUTTON.

> JOE (MACHINE)
> "ARE YOU TRYING TO CHEER ME
> UP?"

> JOHN
> I'm just saying, maybe you
> need to be a little nicer to
> people because — (PISSED TO
> BARTENDER) Hey, what do I
> have to do, go back there and
> make the drink myself? (THEN)
> Where was I?

JOE TYPES.

JOE (MACHINE)
(PUSHES BUTTON) "BEING NICE."

JOHN
You know, if you keep doing
this, Joe, you're gonna push
people away. And you can't
afford to do that.

THE BARTENDER SETS THE DRINK DOWN IN
FRONT OF JOHN.

BARTENDER
Choke on it.

JOHN
Thank you.

THE BARTENDER GRUNTS AND MOVES OFF.

JOHN
(TO JOE) Maybe you should
just be a little more careful
what you say to people. You
know, think about how it's
gonna make them feel. Like
your daughter, for instance.
She might be a little over-
sensitive, she might be a
little, I don't know…

JOHN STOPS WHEN HE SEES JOE TYPING. JOE

PUSHES THE BUTTON.

> JOE (MACHINE)
> "MY DAUGHTER IS NICE TO ME."

> JOHN
> What do you mean? Like overly
> nice to you, because that can
> drive you nuts, too. I got
> people like that in my life…

JOE TYPES AND PRESSES THE BUTTON AGAIN.

> JOE (MACHINE)
> "NO, SHE'S JUST NICE."

> JOHN
> Then, why are you so mean to
> her?

JOE THINKS ABOUT IT FOR A MOMENT AND THEN
TYPES AND PUSHES THE BUTTON.

> JOE (MACHINE)
> "I DON'T KNOW."
> JOHN
> Maybe you're angry at every-
> body and she just happens to
> be in the line of fire?

JOE CONSIDERS THIS, THEN PUSHES THE BUT-
TON AGAIN.

                    JOE (MACHINE)
"I DON'T KNOW."

                         JOHN
So, you think if you're not
nice to people, they're not
gonna miss you when you're
gone? I mean, come on, this
is your daughter we're talking about, Joe…

FINISHES TYPING AND PUSHES THE BUTTON.

                    JOE (MACHINE)
"I DON'T WANT TO LEAVE HER."
(TYPES AND PUSHES BUTTON) "I
LOVE MY DAUGHTER."

                         JOHN
Then don't leave her before
you have to.

JOE THINKS ABOUT THIS A MOMENT. THEN PUTS
HIS HAND ON HIS HEART TO SAY THANK YOU.

                    JOHN (CONT'D)
You're welcome. (A BEAT) You
know, I understand you're
pissed-off about people, but
what do you have against the
dog? I mean, come on, it's
just a dog.

```
JOE TYPES AND PUSHES THE BUTTON.

                    JOE (MACHINE)
          "IT'S A POODLE." (TYPES AN-
          OTHER MESSAGE) "WEARS A
          SWEATER."

                    JOHN
          (LAUGHS) I got it.

THEY TOAST AND DRINK.

                              FADE OUT:
               END OF ACT TWO
```

In the end, I don't know if the episode was good, bad, just tolerable or what. I never know when I'm working on something, and seldom have the courage to go back and look at it afterward. But Ted and Tom's performances that night were moving. Especially since a few of us on the writing staff had been told by someone in Casting that Tom's wife had died of ALS a few years earlier. That wasn't why he took the role; in fact, he never brought it up. But to those of us who knew...the evening was all the more poignant.

On film nights, we writer/producer types usually stood between the 300 or so audience members stacked in the bleachers, and the handful of actors playing pretend on the brightly lit set in front of us. During which, we spent much of our time moving this way or that to avoid the four behemoth cameras that scrambled from one mark to the next on a second's notice. Between takes, we'd huddle to assess the scene, to pitch new jokes, etc., while the warm up guy told the audience stories and jokes, answered questions, danced, performed magic, did whatever he or she could to keep their boredom at bay.

Robert Lee was one of our regular warm ups; a genuinely nice guy and an accomplished comedian (often mutually exclusive qualities). He had gotten to know my dad over the course of the season, since Woody was always in the front row. In fact, he'd often single Woody out and explain the machine to the audience, and then the two of them would fool around with it to make different noises. (There's a "Whiz" sound, an "Uh-oh!" sound and a "Meep! Meep!" Road Runner sound.) It was a great way for Robert to kill some time, and it was fun for my dad.

But on this night, when the episode itself featured the same type of machine, Robert explained that the show's idea was based on Woody, who, like Tom Poston's character, had ALS. By that stage in the filming, the audience was well aware of what ALS was, and now suddenly there, sitting amongst them, was a man for whom the meaning of the words on the stage applied. After the audience knew it, something changed. It was palpable. There was an energy of something...a feeling of connectedness? Even, or especially, in the laughs. It was not uncomfortable, this energy—after all, everything was out in the open, nothing had been denied or left unsaid. Many of us on stage had been feeling it that week, that intensity, but that the audience began to feel the same thing was something I hadn't anticipated. And as Ted and Tom played out the last scenes, the feeling was intense, sustained, like we were all on the verge of crying together, like we all wanted to hug the man sitting in the front row.

For whatever reason, the *Becker* series was never much touted or promoted by the network. During its five-and-a-half-year run, it seemed to float in perpetuity just below the radar. But in the weeks leading up to the airing of the ALS episode, a number of media outlets did pieces on it. *TV Guide* wanted a picture of Ted and Woody together, so the studio sent a driver to pick Woody up at his house and bring him into Paramount for a photo shoot. The photo appeared on a middle page of *TV Guide* describing the episode's background. *E! Entertainment* did a segment with Ted and Tom Poston, plugging the ALS Association and the Muscular Dystrophy Association. Before the interview, Ted came over to me and asked again how to describe the dynamics of the disease, so that he could sound like he knew what he was talking about. "It's when the motor neurons between the muscle groups and the spinal column begin to degenerate." He repeated it a couple of times until he had it right, then moved off and, when the question came up, he delivered the line and sounded very much like he actually knew what he was talking about.

Entertainment Tonight came to the soundstage and interviewed Woody and me in the diner set.

Then they interviewed Ted.

He sat down and made a joke about how, with this episode, Woody had been on the set all the time. "We can't get rid of him, he's everywhere. With that stupid little machine, interrupting me all the time." But when the talk turned more introspective, Ted's demeanor changed. He was quiet for a moment, and then spoke softly. "Here's a man who knows that he has very little time left..." He stopped and turned his head away to clear his throat. Still looking away, he said, "This is a... strange conversation to have, uh..." He forced an uneasy laugh and turned back. "Well, shoot..." he said, unable to finish what he was going to say.

The camera cut away.

A moment later, with the camera back on, Ted turned to the interviewer. "You know, it's so...sweet to see them together," he said, meaning Woody and me. He thought another moment. "Makes me think of my father...in a very loving way."

I remember seeing Ted's father once. In the first year of the show, he'd come by the *Becker* stage to watch a rehearsal. He was in a wheelchair, bald, as I recall, and he looked frail. He died a few months later. For whatever reasons, Ted never got to spend much time with his father during that period, but wished he had, wished he could have. And as he started to get to know my dad, he'd told me several times that he envied the weeks and months we, Woody and I, were spending together. I often felt that much of the affection he shared with Woody and me was his way of reaching out to his own father.

During the week the episode aired, Woody got emails and phone calls from people he hadn't heard from in years. Fortunately, Oleta was back again from Arizona to help out, especially with the calls...and with one request from a friend of mine. Jodi. She wanted an autographed picture of Woody, now that he was "famous." So we scanned and enlarged Woody's Marine

Corps picture and, as Woody started to sign it, I told him to keep it vague, so as not to encourage fans like Jodi who might start stalking him. He laughed, and signed it, "To Jodi! Best Wishes, Woody!"

I framed it and gave it to Jodi the next day.

A few months later, the Muscular Dystrophy Association called to say they were giving their "Super Nova" award to *Becker* for the episode. It would be a black tie gala and dinner in April, with some 800 guests expected...and if Woody wanted to attend, they would provide a limousine for him and a guest.

When I asked him if he was up for it, he raised his thumb and nodded. Only, he added, if I would call his sister and let her know that she would be his guest.

"The face of a child can say it all, especially the mouth part of the face."

Jack Handey, *Deep Thoughts*

SEVEN
Life with Henry and Joe

While nearly every aspect of his life had taken a dramatic turn, the most significant and welcome was the propinquity of his grandsons, and the amount of time he was suddenly able to spend with them.

After Henry and Joe's births, Woody was thrilled with the prospect of having grandchildren, of being a grandfather (my brother never had kids). But, he was pained, I'm sure, to see the boys so seldom in their first few years.

One of the rare trips I'd made out to Pahrump was with Henry, maybe a couple years before my mother's death. Henry was three-and-a-half or four at the time. We were there only a day or so, since it was not a place I was very comfortable. The morning we were leaving, Grampa offered to take Henry out in the back for a ride on the tractor-mower. Henry of course jumped at the opportunity, and off they went. I stood at the sliding glass door and watched as my dad pulled his grandson up onto his lap. I could see him explaining to Henry how everything worked as he fired up the engine and then let Henry take the steering wheel. They were both having a blast.

My mother, meanwhile, had taken a single piece of toast out of the toaster and put it on a plate for me. Breakfast. I sat down at the kitchen counter in front of it. "Thanks," I said, pushing a smile.

"If you want some butter, it's in the fridge," she said, and crossed to the dining room table.

I turned the dry toast over to look at its underside, tossed it back on the plate and got up to get the butter. "Is there any juice?"

"There's milk and prune juice."

"Oh," I said, as I opened the fridge and found a tub of margarine. I could hear the occasional yelps of delight from Henry, as he and his grandfather passed near the house on the tractor-mower.

I buttered the toast and started to eat it, while I struggled through a conversation with my mother about their vacation and how their two dogs loved to travel in the Fifth Wheel (the trailer behind my dad's truck). But Pretty Boy, my mother's parrot, didn't like the trip at all. It made him too tired. Like many things she said, I was vastly unsure what this meant. Why would a bird get tired from traveling? Then she explained that he had to hold on to his perch for the whole trip. Okay, that made sense and, had this bird not been my mortal enemy, I would've worked up some sympathy for him.

As she talked, I noticed that Pretty Boy had hopped down from the windowsill onto the counter, and began to swagger toward me. I knew to keep my distance, ever since I first ran into this bird a few years earlier. At the time, I'd been encouraged by my mother to pet him but, as I moved my finger to gently stroke the side of his head, he turned and locked his jaws around my finger. Until that point, I had no notion of the power inherent in the beak of a parrot. That's when my mother mentioned, with an affectionate laugh, "Oh, that Pretty Boy. Sometimes he bites. And he's *very* strong." Then to him: "Aren't you a strong Pretty Boy?" As tears welled in my eyes, the bird did not let up and showed no signs of intending to do so. He was apparently intent on removing the digit from my hand and I briefly weighed the possible repercussions of using my free hand to grab, say, the fireplace shovel and whack the little fucker in the head. But doing so would have caused bigger problems. Finally, when I moved my other hand up to maybe unlock his jaw, he flinched and let go of my finger. I said something like, wow, that's a fun bird, and edged closer to the fireplace shovel.

So as I sat at the kitchen counter that morning, eating my toast, I kept a cautious eye on this bird while it strolled along the countertop in front of me. He was eyeballing me too, unsure I suppose if he knew me, or maybe, judging by the confidence of his strut, he recognized my finger. When he had finished establishing whose countertop was whose, he turned the other direction, hopped up on the cooling toaster and ambled across the top of it—dropping, as he did, a dollop of shit in one of the bread slots. Honestly. Seriously. As I watched him do this, I didn't say anything, just put the toast back on the plate, figured I'd grab something to eat on the way out of town.

When my father and Henry returned from their

tractor ride, they stepped in through the sliding glass doors and were met by the two dogs, Ace and Heidi. Miniature Pinchers. They were both friendly, but aggressive. Unfortunately, Henry had only the week before been scared by a large dog in the park that knocked him over and pinned him down, only to lick his face, but he was still a little traumatized by the incident.

When I asked my mother if she could put the dogs outside, she sighed, got up and opened the sliding glass door. Ace, the older dog automatically bolted for the backyard, but Heidi the younger one was not so willing. My mother called out to the dog, but for some reason she'd mixed up the names. "Henry! Outside," she yelled. "Outside, Henry! Right now!" Henry, of course, looked a little confused, and when Heidi didn't respond to being called Henry, my mother started to get angry and yelled a little louder. "Henry! I said outside!"

When Henry looked up at me, I smiled and reassured him, "She means the dog."

While my trips out to Pahrump could be counted on one hand (of a cartoon character), my parents' couple of trips to Studio City were strangely brief. On one such occasion, they showed up at our house on a Saturday afternoon, after making the five-hour drive from Nevada. The boys were two and four, and, having already spent a good deal of time with their Australian grandparents, they understood well the purpose of these older relatives: They were a source of limitless loving approval without burdensome prerequisites, and toys.

While my dad was dragged off to the carpet in the living room by Henry and Joe, I struggled to find something to talk about with my mother. Cath managed to avoid the same dilemma by drifting off to the kitchen to make lunch for the boys. I thought my mother would be excited about seeing how big Henry and Joe were getting; that Henry was a walking encyclopedia of "el-phants," and Joe had transformed from a slobbering infant to a bruising toddler. But she seemed disinterested as she sat down with me on the steps between the dining room and the living room.

Meanwhile, Henry and Joe were waiting patiently for my dad to finish discarding obtrusive items like his glasses and his watch, to empty his pockets of change, to put his keys and his wallet aside. When he moved to his hands and knees and told them he was ready, the assault came swiftly and without mercy; Henry climbing up onto his shoulders and his back, as Joe came from the other side trying to do the same. They were both squealing and laughing, as they struggled to ride this wild horse. And as they clung to his neck and wormed their way across his back, giggling the whole time and demanding that he move here or there, I was struck by the sound of my dad's laughter. It was hearty, full. It was robust, the kind of laughter that rose from the heart; the kind that said not only how much he loved rolling around on the floor with them, but how much he loved them. Or could, given the time. At one point he looked up to me, feigning that it was too much, that he needed help. I shook my head and said he'd gotten himself into this mess, he could get himself out.

As it turned out, he didn't have to. After a few minutes of roughhousing, my mother stood and announced that it was time to go.

They'd been at the house a total of thirty minutes.

Catherine shot me a confused look, as even I was a little surprised.

My father looked disappointed, but peeled off the clinging boys, replaced his wallet and keys, his glasses and watch, and stood up to say good-bye. They got back in the truck and made the five-hour drive back to Pahrump.

Why he didn't just say no to her on that and many occasions was a perennial mystery to me. I suspect it had to do with an attrition of resolve over the many years they'd been together. As well, it may have been his realization that doing so, resisting, would be met with limitless anger. And her anger, once piqued, could not be bested or brought to reason. So his choice to acquiesce was wiser maybe, or at least easier.

By the time Woody was living in Studio City and seeing his grandsons almost daily, he could no longer speak at all. It was something the boys took in stride, the way children do. They, like their friends at school—who all came to know Woody—would ask him a question and simply wait for an answer from the LightWRITER.

On Saturday afternoons, during the boys' soccer games, he'd sit in his collapsible chair on the grass beside the field, and kids would often come up to him and ask to hear their names on the LightWRITER. He'd type their names, push the button and smile at their laughter. And when they wanted to hear more, silly words mostly, he'd hand over the machine so they could type them out themselves. Once in a while, a kid would ask him, "How come you can't talk?" And Joe or Henry would say, "He's got ALS." And though none I'm sure knew what ALS was, that was enough.

More often than not, though, Woody didn't need the LightWRITER to communicate with his grandsons. They seemed to understand Grampa more from a look or a motion, perhaps because much of their relationship was tactile. Since they were so often sitting on Grampa's lap or holding his hand, I'm sure it lent itself to a more innate ability to sense his intent. When we were out in public—like the many trips we'd made to Target to get things for his new house—I noticed that Henry, then almost six, was developing something of a tutelary relationship with him. If I moved off with Catherine and Joe, Henry would hang back with Grampa, and hold his hand like he was looking out for him.

When the boys expressed interest in a fort—having seen photos of the one my dad built for me when I was their age—Woody set about building them one in his backyard. He had not yet started to lose strength in his hands and legs, so the construction was fairly easy for him. He dug holes and poured concrete foundations for the 4X4 stilts that would support the structure. He built a ladder that ascended through a small trap door at the floor of the fort. Then he built a roof, complete with shingles.

After he finished the construction and painting (it matched the house), he decided he wasn't finished. When Joe or Henry mentioned that it was their "spaceship," Woody typed out to me, "JUNKYARD."

I squinted at him, not sure what he meant.

He typed, "NEED SEATS FOR SPACESHIP."

The following Saturday, the four of us drove to South

Los Angeles, and scoured the twisted iron graveyards of mangled cars and trucks, looking for some bucket seats. When we found two that looked good, I was astounded to find out that the junkyard wanted $160 for them. I stood in front of the crisscrossing wrought iron bars and the grungy window of the cashier within, and squinted at the guy like he was kidding. "A hundred-and-sixty bucks? Seriously? Because...they're not new. I mean, the last people who used them probably went through the windshield." My dad, though, moved me aside and handed the man his credit card.

After the boys and I managed to lug the seats out to my car and wrestle them into a semi-legal position for transport, we realized that Woody was still on the grounds of the junkyard, poking around the wreckage. When I found him and said we were ready to go, he typed, "STEERING WHEEL."

I sighed in resignation and said, "Well, yeah, okay, I guess a spaceship needs a steering wheel."

After the seats had been bolted to the floor of the "spaceship" and the steering wheel attached to the railing, the boys and their friends, Timmy and Connor from next door, took up residence. When I wandered from the backyard out to the garage, I found Woody cutting the wooden pole of a market umbrella in two. I asked what he was doing, and he stopped long enough to type, "LASER GUNS."

I looked at him like he had perhaps lost his mind.

He slipped PVC piping, the joining sections, over the barrel-end of the "guns," and they looked like muzzles. Then he attached the handles from a couple of old hacksaws to serve as handles. Once assembled, the guns were mounted on swivels from metal wheelbases (sans the wheels), so that they could be turned to shoot in any direction. Now the spaceship could protect itself on its many journeys across the cosmos.

Since he hadn't seen the boys much before my mother's death, he delighted in hearing stories about them when they were younger. Especially the small stories, the funny ones that—as I look back—gave glimpses of who Henry and Joe would become, none more so than this one about Henry and the cat.

When he was about three, I had climbed into his bed early one morning and lay down beside him to sleep for a while. (After Joe's arrival, Henry had been moved temporarily into a queen-sized bed, freeing up his old crib for Joe.) During which our orange cat, Earl Lempky, joined us and sprawled out across the middle of the bed with that innate sense of feline ownership. After a while, Henry woke and decided to get up, but he had been essentially boxed in by Earl and me. I roused when I heard him trying to get the cat's attention. As I lay listening, my eyes still closed, I was taken by how polite he was being to the cat.

"Excuse me, kitty," he whispered gently. "Excuse me." I could feel him tugging lightly on the comforter, trying not to jolt the cat out of a deep sleep. Earl though wasn't moving. So Henry continued. "Excuse me, kitty. Kitty? Excuse me." He tugged a couple more times on the comforter and continued his delicate entreaties. "Kitty? Excuse me, please."

Finally, Earl lifted his head, rolled an annoyed eye at Henry, stood, stretched and jumped off the bed.

Henry then turned at me. "Daddy?"

"Huh?"

"Move."

The story confirmed for me who this little person was and would be—respectful to the smaller souls of the universe, while affording the larger ones little latitude—an iconoclast who treats his underlings with deference.

He was, and is, I realized, what I have always aspired to become.

Joe and the same cat.

Catherine and Earl had their differences. She was never a fan and expressed her disdain freely. To a large degree, this relationship came about because Earl, for some reason, felt a need to urinate on her unattended clothes, whether he found them folded and neatly stacked, or lying haphazardly on the floor of the bedroom. That he was a pseudo family member was perhaps the only thing that, on several occasions, saved his life.

Cath was at work one day when Joe and I went into the kitchen to make a couple of sandwiches. He was about three-and-a-half years old and as many feet tall. As I opened the fridge, Earl sauntered in and jumped up on the kitchen's island—where he was not supposed to be.

"Earl, get down!" I said as I shooed him off. "You know better than that."

As Earl moved to the side of the countertop and jumped down, I heard Joe's tiny voice beside me. "Fucking cat."

He'd obviously heard the expression before. I was a little surprised. I looked down at him. He returned the look and added an ingenuous, "What?"

Several times, when Woody had friends over and the subject of his grandsons came up, he'd implore me, "TELL THE 'FUCKING CAT' STORY."

There were obvious advantages with Woody living so close, none more apparent or appreciated than when he came over to build or fix things: the garage door, the sprinkler system, new shelves in the boys' bedroom, storage racks in the garage. It was also walking distance between the two houses. Or, in Henry and Joe's case, bicycle-riding distance (in the company of an adult).

On one particular summer evening, we were, Henry, Joe and I, returning from watching a movie over at Grampa's house. It was dusk, and he'd offered to stick the bikes in his car and drive us home. I said it wasn't necessary, we'd gotten ourselves there, we'd get ourselves back.

The boys rode their bikes. I was walking. It was a balmy night as we passed through the neighborhood under the dome of the giant elms. From one languid street to the next, unseen crickets chirped to the distant hum of traffic from Laurel Canyon Boulevard.

Unfortunately, in my ever-evolving approach to fatherhood, I'd decided that Henry was becoming too cautious in his day-to-day choices. Joe, on the other hand, by age four, had twice—at two different birthday parties—decided to run full-bore at an open swimming pool, causing Catherine to twice jump fully clothed into those swimming pools to rescue him. Don't get me wrong, I didn't want either of the boys to do dangerous things, but I (perhaps unwisely) wanted each to embrace a little more of the other's attitude. Which is not to say that I thought children could be molded into something they're not. In fact, if there was ever an argument for the tenacity of the soul (and perhaps even reincarnation), it is the way these small beings emerge and seem to be already who they are.

That said, I thought I could *influence* Henry, just a little, to be slightly more daring.

Certainly he knew how to speak up for himself. *That* I was not concerned about. Once, while strapped to his booster seat in the back of Catherine's car, the setting sun on the 101 West was hitting him squarely in the eyes. Not one to put up with something so annoying, he began screaming at the top of his lungs, "Move the sun! Move the sun! MOVE THE...SUN!"

Within the family, the expression is still referenced.

Nor have I ever been concerned about Henry's resolve when he sets his mind on something. That became glaringly clear to me one Saturday morning when he was two-and-a-half and had just poured a box of Cheerios on the kitchen floor. He knew it was wrong, and I knew he knew it was wrong, even if he was only two-and-a-half. I told him he was not leaving the kitchen until he picked all of it up. He informed me then that he had no intention of doing so. A little stymied by his firm stand, I let him know that he wasn't leaving the kitchen until he did. He repeated that he wasn't going to pick up the Cheerios, so we sat down on opposite sides of the mess; he with stark defiance in his eyes and heart, his little arms folded in front of him; me, on the other side of the cereal, beginning to fear that I'd bitten off more than I could chew.

At his age, I figured he was good for five, maybe ten minutes.

The face-off continued for the next half hour, then forty minutes, forty-five, fifty minutes. As the clock edged past one hour, it occurred to me that I might be spending the rest of my weekend on the floor of the kitchen. After an hour and change, he resigned himself finally to pick up the cereal, while I breathed a sigh of relief and quietly decided to choose my future battles more carefully.

So, no, I had no concerns about Henry's "resolve."

I just felt that he needed to be a little less afraid of trying things, new things, like broccoli and the Beatles, and maybe even some things that seemed a little risky. It was a ridiculous concern, in hindsight, for a plethora of reasons, not the least of which was what took place on our way home from Grampa's house that night.

I saw, as we approached each sidewalk from the street, Henry would get off his bicycle and lift it up onto the sidewalk, walk it a ways and then he'd get back on the bike. I mentioned to him that he should try popping his front wheel up as he rode toward the sidewalk. Then he'd be able to keep riding without getting off the bike.

He thought about it and said, "Nah, I don't think so. I'll just get off the bike and lift it."

"Okay, but when you do it that way, Henry, you have to stop and get off the bike. My way is faster."

"I don't mind," he said, and started to ride off.

"Okay, hold on, hold on!" I yelled to him as he rode away. "Come here, come here. Gimme the bike."

He stopped and looked at me.

"Come on, get off the bike."

A sigh. Reluctantly he relinquished it and stood next to Joe, while I hunched down and pedaled the tiny bike out into the street to show them both how it was done.

It was a wide intersection at a confluence of several streets. No cars around. Here and there, front windows glowed with amber light from kitchens with dinners being prepared. I used the width of the street to circle and gain speed before I came swooping in on the curb like a majestic falcon over skittering prey, jerking the handle bars at precisely the right moment to pop the front wheel up. The scene shifted then to slow-motion, as the bike's front wheel did indeed pop up, but was followed by the rest of the bike as it flew out from under me and off toward someone's shrubbery. From mid-air, I watched, as it floated away and I floated back toward the street, landing, ass first, my elbows diving into the asphalt like torpedoes, my head jerking back, my neck jolting from the weight of my head.

It was bad.

As I lay supine in the street, searing pain shooting through my neck and back, my elbows, my ass, everything, I wondered if I'd snapped something important like, say, my spine. I flashed on a future of wheelchairs and tubes and incontinence. And buying another house, since the one we lived in was chockablock with stairs. I noticed then that Henry and Joe had walked over, and were standing on either side of me, looking down at me like two birds examining a turd in their feeder. After a moment, Henry looked up and across to Joe. "Boy," he said, "that was stupid."

One could conclude that the experience, up to that point, was more than enough humiliation for one father. But as I hobbled the rest of the way home and Henry rode his bike (stopping at each sidewalk curb to lift it), Joe decided to walk his bike beside me. While I picked small rocks out of my bleeding elbows, he apparently felt a need to point out a lesson that should not go unrealized. "You know, Dad, big people aren't supposed to ride little people's bikes."

"Uh-huh."

"Because it's very dangerous."

"Yeah, I realize that, Joe. Thanks."

"If you're a big person and you ride a little person's bike, you can get in a wreck," he said.

"Right, Joe, I got it."

"Little people don't ride big people's bikes..."

"Yes, I know that."

"Because, if they do, they can get hurt."

"Right," I said.

"And a big person is too big for a little person's bike."

While Henry rode quietly along beside us, no doubt satisfied that his method of transitioning to sidewalks was infinitely more prudent than his father's, Joe continued to make what he felt was a salient point. "Little people's bikes are made for little people to ride. Not big people."

"I understand that, Joe, yes, thank you," I said.

"If you're a big person, you should be riding a big person's bike."

I'd never seen him so goddamn focused. "Yes, yes," I said, hoping he was done.

"Because big people are too big for—"

"Joe! Yes. I got it."

"Okay," he said.

When we got home, the boys, now invigorated by a wildly exciting story, gleefully regaled it to Catherine—confirmation for her that she'd married an idiot. The next day Woody seemed to take particular delight in its telling by Joe and Henry (complete with pantomimed reenactments). And when Oleta returned from the grocery store (she was back again for another visit), Woody insisted the boys tell the story to her. And then, of course, when the boys' nanny Claudia came by in the late afternoon to pick them up, Woody got Henry's attention and typed: "TELL THE BIKE STORY."

"It goes so fast, Grampa. So fast!" Joe said one day with an enthusiasm that was nearly an open challenge to doubt him. "You're not gonna believe how fast this goes!"

Woody was sitting on the couch in our living room, while Joe stood before him making this bold declaration. He was holding a toy steering wheel that his Grampa had given him for Christmas. It had a horn in its center and some buttons on the side that made a variety of engine noises. It wasn't mounted on anything, wasn't part of anything else, it was just a steering wheel that made noise. That's it.

"You don't believe me?" Joe said, confronting an imagined challenge to his claim. "Watch this!" Then he pushed the button that started up the car's engine, and took off running as fast as he could, circling the couch again and again, running, running...until finally he came to a stop in front of his grandfather, winded, but deadly serious and triumphant in his assertion. "Pretty fast, huh, Grampa?" he said, regaining his breath. I don't know if that is the hardest I'd seen my dad laugh, but if not, it was close.

Woody clearly got a kick out of hearing his grandsons explain their days, express their theories about this or that. He would lean back in his black leather chair and listen intently to their observations and opinions—no matter how askew.

When Joe informed his grandfather that his favorite animal in the world was the chicken, my dad looked surprised. (Henry's choice, as you know, was the "el-phant"—a magnificent creature in many regards, and understandably a child's favorite in the animal kingdom. Joe's choice, however, was a far less obvious one. The barnyard chicken doesn't bring to mind the grace, the speed or ferocity of the usual iconic creatures that children obsess about—cheetahs streaking across an open plane, eagles soaring overhead, whales cresting the ocean's surface. But, for Joe...it was the chicken.) So after Joe made this proud announcement, Woody typed, "WHY?" Joe scrunched his face as though the answer should be obvious to anyone. "'Cause," he said, "they're so stupid you can catch 'em!"

As any parent knows, there is hardly a greater joy than sharing the pleasures and fascinations of our youth with our offspring. I had long remembered a movie that transfixed me when I was a kid. It was Jerry Lewis's 1960 masterpiece, *Cinderfella.* I remember seeing it several times, anticipating anxiously its showing whenever I learned it was going to be on TV.

This was a cinematic experience I was determined

to share with the boys.

The trouble was no stores had copies of it; there was nothing on Netflix; nothing online, nothing except on eBay. So I made a bid on a videotape copy and easily won. When it arrived, I gathered the boys at Grampa's house to revel in it.

I had of course talked it up quite a bit, telling Joe and Henry how much they were absolutely going to get such a kick out of this movie. "It's so funny when Jerry Lewis turns his socks inside out and paints them black so he can get into the ball!" I said as I shoved the tape into the machine and sat on the floor with Henry and Joe, while my dad looked on from his desk chair. "You guys are gonna love this movie."

For the first five or ten minutes of the film, Jerry Lewis makes orange juice. He had been told to do so by his evil stepmother. Yes, he was a genius at physical comedy, but how many ways, and for how long, can you drag out the screwing up of the making of orange juice?

"Okay, I don't remember this part, but it gets better," I told the boys and Woody, who were starting to fidget.

It never got better.

I don't know what it was, don't know why I was so enamored with this movie when I was a kid. Perhaps, over the course of forty years, my taste—though some might quibble—had matured. Basically *Cinderfella* was a string of physical bits, with Lewis bumping his way through one whacky, pointlessly protracted antic after the next—more often than not, those antics having little to do with the progression of the story. Henry and Joe were six and four—*they* were too mature for it.

The boys did their best to be polite about the whole

thing, but twenty minutes in, Henry stood and said he was going out to play with the dog. The idea appealed to Joe, too, who got up and went out with him. And as the glass door slid closed behind them, I turned to my dad and saw that he'd typed something on the LightWRITER. He pushed the button and it said: "GREAT MOVIE."

The big bathtub downstairs in our house was broken again. I tried to fix it, but knew before I started, it was futile. The toggle knob that plugs the tub wasn't working, so the only way to plug up the water was the old fashioned way, with a rubber stopper in the drain. When I mentioned it to my dad one evening on my way home from work, I knew he'd be over at the house soon with a doctor bag of tools.

Sure enough, when I got home the next day, his car was out front. As I dropped my backpack in the kitchen and said hi to Cath, I heard clanking downstairs. She said he was in our bathroom, fixing the tub. I padded downstairs, through our bedroom and into the bathroom, where Woody was kneeling in the oversized belly of the empty tub with the tub's internal components pulled out of the hole beneath the faucet. He was trying to attach one of the more intricate parts to another, and probably would have had the whole thing done by the time I'd gotten home, except...Joe was helping.

While Henry, at six, had already figured out that other people's problems belonged to other people—Joe, at four, had become the perennial "helper." Apparently, when he found out that Grampa was in the bathroom working on the tub, he could not be talked out of assisting in the effort. And there he was, standing beside my dad in the tub, offering advice and insisting on helping Grampa get all of the assembled pieces back into the tub's opening.

"Hey, Dad...thanks," I said, stepping into the tub and sitting on its edge. "Hiya, Joe. Helping Grampa, are ya?"

"Yeah," Joe said quickly without looking up, too focused on the work at hand.

With Joe's "help," Woody was having trouble getting the attached pieces back in place. I asked if I could do anything. Woody slid the pieces back out of the hole and picked up the LightWRITER to type: "FLASHLIGHT."

"Oh, sure," I said, and went off to track one down. When I returned and handed the flashlight to him, he gave it to Joe, indicating to him where the light needed to be directed. Joe, now engaged in a more official capacity, was happy to oblige. He turned the flashlight on and began his task in earnest. As I sat and watched, I realized that the light itself wandered frequently from its target, but it didn't seem to matter to Woody, as he slid the components back into the hole and managed to get the whole thing reattached and working.

"Nice, Dad," I said when I walked him out to his car.

He looked at me.

"The flashlight," I said. "Very smart. Great way to get Joe out of the way."

He smiled, and reached for the LightWRITER. "MY HELPER," he typed.

I was impressed with his diplomacy and supportive nature, his sense of kindness and patience. And his inventiveness. After all, he'd managed not to stifle the good intentions of a persistent grandson, bent on "helping" come hell or high water.

It wasn't until I stood on the front lawn, watching the taillights of his car disappear around the corner that it occurred to me how frequently in *my* childhood I had been out in the garage helping him, and he would ask me to hold the flashlight.

When my brother Phil came to visit—it turned out to be the only time he would do so—Woody put him to work on his next project. When I stopped by the house, Phil was in the garage with him, helping build two plywood-topped tables.

"What're you doing?"

"FOR SLOT CARS," Woody typed.

He'd decided to turn his living room into a slot car track.

The tables were huge and had to be moved into the living room in sections before they were reassembled. The living room furniture was moved to the side or out of the room, as the two tables together took up a great deal of space. Once attached to each other, they were covered with grass-like green paper, the type used to build little towns for miniature trains.

A couple of days later, we drove to a train store in Burbank that sold slot cars and slot car track. Woody bought a couple of fast-looking cars and several hundred dollars worth of track. And by the time it was put together, it was a twisting, turning, looping black ribbon that banked off one end of the conjoined tables and streaked to the other, where it whipped around and into another set of tortuous curves, an underpass, and into a straight-away that stretched the length of the room. And then it did it all again.

It was beautiful.

The next thing I knew, he was out in the backyard, spraying out heaps of insulation foam onto a spread newspaper. When I asked what he was doing, what it was for, he stopped and typed out, "MOUNTAINS." Then he took a can of brown spray paint and started spraying the drying mounds of foam. And they were mountains. One of them even surrounded a small mirror—a lake.

"Goddamn, Dad," I said, truly impressed, "that looks great."

He smiled.

I went into the house and got something to drink. But as I stepped back out into the yard, something occurred to me. "You know..." I said as he put the paint can down and I approached, "you never made anything like this for me."

He thought about it and typed: "TOUGH."

Over the next couple of weeks, he ended up making several more trips to the train store to buy more scenery and a lap counter. The track became something of a gathering point for boys and men. Yes, women saw it— Cath, Claudia the nanny, Oleta, Kerri the neighbor, Sonia (our housekeeper) and other female friends—and they mentioned how lucky Joe and Henry were to have such a great racetrack. But their eyes didn't light up the way ours did, we boys, we men. Yes, he'd built it for his grandsons, but none of us, none of my friends, had ever had anything like it. In fact, there were often accusations by the younger boys that the grown-up boys were hogging the slot car track. Of course, the older boys were frequently clutching not just a slot car's throttle, but a can of beer, which gave them, us, the necessary courage to ignore the little complainers.

And when Henry and Joe did get to use it and took a corner too fast and wiped out against the wall or the railing, they'd pick up the broken pieces and hand them to Grampa for repair. And he'd retire to his black leather chair at his desk in the TV room, and one or the other of the boys would get the necessary tools and parts from the credenza, and then would pull himself up onto Grampa's lap, and Grampa would set about repairing the car.

Inevitably, it was decided that the two slot cars were not enough. Or it may have been that one of the cars was so damaged after sailing into the wall that it was declared irreparable. So again we were off to the train store in Burbank. This time though, the boys were coming with us to make sure the correct choices were made.

Interestingly, Henry and Joe were going through a phase where they preferred getting into my car by means of the trunk—since the back seat flipped down, allowing them access to the cabin. As we walked out to the car, a neighbor, Michelle, was watering her lawn. She yelled hi to my dad as she wagged the hose from side to side. He turned and waved, while I opened the trunk to let Henry and Joe climb in. When I closed it behind them, I noticed that Michelle had cocked her head curiously. I shrugged to her like, "Crazy kids like using the trunk." It wasn't until we were driving away that I realized—with the car's tinted windows—Michelle could only have assumed that my dad and I were driving off with the boys in the trunk.

When I mentioned it to Woody, he laughed and typed, "I'LL WATCH FOR COPS."

Many times in the latter stages of Woody's illness, when I could see in his eyes the weight of his dwindling time was all but drowning him, we'd hear a car door slam in the driveway and the house's front door bang open and one or two little voices squawk, "Grampa!" And suddenly his eyes would brighten, knowing he was soon to be assaulted by the small clinging hands of Henry or Joe climbing onto his lap.

They alone managed to breathe life into him.

While he had not been a part of their past, could not be a part of their future—they were very much his present. They were two sparks of light that kept him focused on other things. And when one or the other took hold of his hand or dropped an arm around his neck, and told him the swirling details of their world, he was shielded from the looming darkness that hung over his.

EIGHT
New Friends

"Oh, my God!" a lesbian friend of mine said, suddenly standing up in the backyard of my dad's house. "I'm so sick of people saying they're practically gay except for the sex! Jesus Christ! You're *not* a dyke unless you eat some goddamn pussy!"

It was a pleasant summer evening in early July. Woody had only just moved into his new neighborhood. A number of friends had come over to meet my dad and see the house. A handful of us, five or six, were sitting on lawn chairs in the backyard with spindly paper plates on our knees, topped with mac & cheese, Sun Chips, a hot dog or hamburger.

And there was Woody.

It was funny, the proclamation made by my gay friend, because it was in response to something said innocently by someone who wasn't gay. (He had mentioned that he was *practically* gay, but for the sex.) And as everyone was about to laugh at the "eating pussy" comment, they suddenly became aware that my father was sitting amongst them—a man in his seventies they barely knew. It was a painfully uncomfortable moment, most everyone just hoping someone would move the conversation forward, until...Woody burst out laughing and, like the release of a pinched balloon, everyone cracked up. And breathed.

Woody was living well within an unfamiliar culture. But as one month gave way to the next, the gap between his former world and his new began to shrink.

After the death of my mother, he'd reconnected with a number of his old friends. His work buddies, family and family friends, all seemed to emerge as though he'd suddenly joined *Facebook* (which was not to show up for another three years). By and large, though, the bulk of his friendships during this period were with younger people; his neighbors, my work associates, my friends—many of whom are gay. It was a new phenomenon for him, this association. A disparate coupling. After all, he was a veteran of WWII, a U.S. Marine at that; he'd grown up in Texas during the Depression. And he was a Republican...though, in fairness, this was well before the Republican Party took the dramatic shift it has taken in the years since.

Suddenly he'd found himself thrust into the middle of a world chockablock with ardent liberals, Democrats, environmentalists, union members, animal rights activists and gay people.

Though I made it a point not to discuss politics with him after he lost his ability to speak—it seemed like an unfair fight—he was surrounded by the living embodiments of my political beliefs. And, while I don't know if any of his political views of the world changed, I know his view of gay people did. How could it not? It is one thing to see a group of people from a distance, as though spectral images in the wavering distance. But to know a person, someone intelligent and kind, someone who has had to endure the hatred of strangers, who has seen an otherwise loving mother or father, brother or sister, look at them with contempt, someone who knows the pain of learning that he or she is no longer welcome in the home where they grew up...well, it can change a person's perspective.

During the long months of his illness, he experienced an outpouring of kindness and compassion from many. But from none was this kindness and compassion more profound and heartfelt than from those friends of mine who are gay. There was a gentleness, a nurturing quality that came into play. Perhaps it is genetic or maybe it's because being gay demands introspection and self-assessment. It demands a certain awareness of the world, and frequently an intimate understanding and recognition of pain in others. It brings with it, very often, sensitivity.

Whatever it is, whatever it was, Woody, in the last months of his life, became pro-gay, as was evident in the quiet joke between us that we would share whenever the subject cropped up: He would cup his hand and wave as though sitting atop a parade float. The Princess Wave. The joke emerged from a discussion about a West Hollywood gay pride parade—an event that one of my gay friends was disgusted by, claiming, "It's nothing but freaks showing off how gay they are!" When I mentioned to my dad that, since he had by then so many gay friends, he should be on one of the floats in the parade, Woody laughed and raised his cupped hand to give me his best Princess Wave.

Among the friends of mine he'd become friends with was a man named Gary Dontzig.

I'd met Gary in the fall of 1988—after the pilot of *Murphy Brown* had been shot, and before a second episode had been conceived—when the writers of the show all sat down together for the first time to have lunch and introduce ourselves. There were seven of us, including Diane English, the show's creator and Executive Producer. We were at a large table in the back of the Warner Brothers' commissary in Burbank.

Gary was ten years older than I and looked remarkably, I thought, like Alan Alda. When it was his turn to introduce himself, he did so by saying he was gay and that he had been in a relationship for 20 years.

Afterwards, I pulled him aside to say how much I appreciated his candor. This was the late '80s after all, and there were (are) still sections of the country where doing so could get a person killed. It was the start of an enduring friendship that thrives still today. A friendship enhanced by the kindness that Gary and his partner, also named Gary, showed my father. (Gary and Gary, by the way, became Henry and Joe's Godparents.)

Dontzig is the type of guy who is constantly preparing a warm meal for a neighbor who isn't feeling well. He was once an hour late for a dinner that Catherine and I were also attending because, when he stopped to get gas, there was a woman sitting inside the accompanying store, near the cash register, weeping. So he sat down with her to talk, to see what was wrong, to help her. When he's on his way somewhere, he won't drive past a stray dog. He has to stop, corral it and find its owner. Or adopt it himself. In fact, the reason for both his and Gary Campbell's veganism was their compassion for animals.

Gary Campbell had been an actor in New York in the late '60s. He was ruggedly handsome, with a chiseled jaw, outlined perennially by emerging stubble. He was a product of the sun-swept wide-open contours of New Mexico's ruddy terrain. He was the Marlboro Man, sans the Marlboro.

Before coming to terms with his homosexuality and meeting Gary Dontzig, Campbell had been married to actress Marsha Mason—who went on to meet, marry (and then divorce) Neil Simon. And by the time *Murphy Brown* began, the Garys (as they were known by friends) and Marsha had solidified a long-standing and caring relationship. It was, from my perspective, a near-marriage amongst three friends. To wit, when a group of us from *Murphy Brown* went rafting down the Colorado River together one April after filming, Gary, Gary and Marsha shared responsibilities and a platonic tent, as though any alternative would have been absurd.

In the mid '90s, Marsha moved from Los Angeles to New Mexico, after buying the equivalent of a valley near Abiquiu, a small town north of Santa Fe. The house she built there was beautiful, of course, Spanish, functional and sprawling—it had to be, considering the horde of dogs that comprised her veritable family. And on a section of land some 90 feet away—overlooking a lowland that swept across the valley to a copse of trees lining a winding river at the foot of the surrounding mountains—the Garys built their own house. It was there that Catherine and I spent a handful of holidays before, and later with, the boys. It was there that we were invited by Gary to spend what would be Woody's last Thanksgiving.

My dad had not yet met Gary Campbell, since Campbell lived fulltime in New Mexico. Dontzig was still working on *Murphy Brown* and later *Suddenly Susan*, so he flew back and forth from Albuquerque to Los Angeles.

From the moment we arrived, my dad felt comfortable around Gary Campbell. Campbell was a guy's guy who worked the land and seemed only to care about being and staying in New Mexico, tending to the land and the many animals that lived there. He was opinionated, with a salt-of-the-earth gruffness that showed little if any patience for politics or the minutiae of society. I recall him, on more than a few occasions, learning about some new celebrity gossip or the latest gadget everybody *had* to have, and he'd lean back in his chair and say it's "all a lot of goddamn bullshit."

The more Campbell would give his all-encompassing disapproval of this or that, the more my dad seemed to like him. Woody would either laugh and nod his head at Campbell's disparaging remark, whatever it was, or type out his concurrence. As they got to know each other better, Campbell would make a condemnation of some public figure, look at my dad and say, "It's horseshit. The guy's an asshole. Am I right, Woody?" And Woody would nod and shoot him a thumbs up to say he was of like mind.

Late on the first day, my dad pulled me aside, nodded toward Campbell with a smile, and then typed, "REMINDS ME OF MY DAD." Though I never met my grandfather, I knew what he meant. Roy Woody died in the early fifties from an otherwise treatable stomach ulcer because he'd refused to see any bullshit doctors who "find things" so they can gouge you out of every last penny you've got!

Thanksgiving was a bustling day between the two houses. The dinner itself was to take place at Marsha's, with a full spread of all the classics: a plump and enormous turkey, mountains of fluffy stuffing, thick gravy, steaming mashed potatoes, string beans, cranberry sauce, real and canned. And there was plenty of not-so-traditional food, since the Garys didn't eat meat or dairy products of any kind. Tofurky, fake bacon, soy in a variety of forms. Most of it surprisingly edible.

There were perhaps ten guests in all, friends of Marsha's who lived in the area, knew her from her business downtown, along with some New York replants in the Santa Fe area. And Shirley MacLaine. She owned a large stretch of property a few miles away. In fact, it was Shirley who told Marsha about Abiquiu, that there was land for sale near the river.

We sat down to a sweeping and bountiful Thanksgiving table—the boys of course relegated to the proverbial Little Person's Table. (I was tempted to point out to Joe that Little Persons couldn't sit at the Big Person's Table because it was too dangerous—but I refrained.) It was a beautiful splay, all of it mouthwatering, its savory tendrils wafting up like warm fingers...none of which Woody could eat. He could still, at that point, get some liquefied foods down, so we'd brought along our little Cuisinart to whip up an assortment of Thanksgiving combos.

And though conversations with Shirley generally extended no further than Shirley, Woody was nonetheless a little flabbergasted to be having dinner with both Marsha Mason and Shirley MacLaine.

Later in the kitchen, Shirley slid an arm over Woody's shoulder for a couple of pictures. And, when we returned home to Studio City, Woody passed the pictures on to his two best friends, Noel and Elmer, with a note explaining that he had a new girlfriend.

While ALS is insidious in its creeping acquisition of the body—its gradual and cruel denial of one function after the next—selfishly it afforded me precious time to be with my father before he was gone. Gary Dontzig was not so "fortunate" with Gary Campbell. A mere three weeks after my father died, Gary Campbell did so suddenly and unexpectedly in the shower one evening at their New Mexico home. Dontzig was in Los Angeles. Campbell's body was not discovered until the following morning when he didn't show up to meet Marsha for their diurnal walk with the dogs. The water of the shower was still running. The Garys' dogs were sitting at the bathroom door, waiting for him to get up.

"Russ?"

"Yeah?"

"It's Gary. Listen, I'm calling some people. Uh...I'm going out to New Mexico. Gary died last night."

I was stunned. "Gary died?"

Though no autopsy was done, the conclusion drawn was that he died of an aneurysm.

I flew out a day or two later to help Dontzig with phone calls and the routine things that needed to be dealt with when someone dies. I had just missed a week of work with the death of my dad, and then I was flying off to New Mexico to do this. But Dontzig had been around so much at the end of my dad's life that I had to do something to help, however little it was.

And while my dad's death was expected and nearly appreciated, Gary Campbell's death hit like a bolt of lightning. It was devastating for both Gary and Marsha. As it was for all of us who loved the Garys.

Of the many relationships in this world that struggle to keep their heads above water, the relationships that smolder with animosity, that succumb to perpetual love-lessness, that implode and disintegrate—theirs was a profound exception. An exception that, for 34 years, exemplified mutual respect, the sincerity of kind intent, love, trust, honor. It was as honest and committed a relationship as I have ever witnessed, straight or gay. Though papers were never drawn, *could not* be drawn, theirs was a marriage that worked, and worked well.

It was maybe two years before Gary Dontzig could refer to Gary Campbell without becoming emotional. During that time, there were legal battles to be fought because, in the eyes of the state—and some of Gary Campbell's relatives—theirs was not a legitimate rela-tionship.

During Woody's time with the Garys, I don't know if it occurred to him to contrast his marriage—a union fully sanctioned by the state—to the Garys' relationship. But I know his affection for Gary and Gary had an effect on his transition to the man waving from the top of a float in the Gay Pride Parade.

Dontzig, now in his seventies, is still single. He says he's not looking for another relationship, jokes that there's no market for an "old fag" like him. Though I think the truth may more be that he feels the lasting satisfaction of a rare and successful relationship.

"For myself I am an optimist—it does not seem to be much use to be anything else."

Winston Churchill

NINE
A Little Bit of Hope

"You know about stem cell research, right?"

"No, I don't know anything about it," I said to Deena, my co-worker, as we stood outside the *Becker* production offices, taking a break.

"When they introduce stem cells into the body, the cells transform into whatever it is the body needs," she said. "They're gonna be able to use it on people with ALS, Parkinson's, Alzheimer's, MS, spinal cord injuries."

"Seriously?"

"Seriously. Look it up."

At Johns Hopkins University, laboratory mice were being bred with symptoms that mimicked ALS. The paralyzed mice had then been injected with embryonic stem cells. Miraculously the stem cells either replaced or regenerated the dying motor neurons of the mice, so that they were able to regain the use of their limbs.

I learned from another source that researchers were within a year of trying it out on humans. Though most estimates weren't nearly so optimistic—some dismissing the idea altogether—it was still a small ray of light in a vast sea of darkness. "Within a year" made the idea tangible, reachable. It was something to hold onto—no matter how pie in the sky it was.

When I told Woody, we both decided to believe.

I copied file after file from websites, called researchers and clipped articles from newspapers and magazines to pass on to him. He meanwhile kept a "Stem Cell" binder and ran off reports from an online news group that relayed stories about embryonic stem cell research. We held tight, blindly at times, to its promise. The search for new and encouraging information was for me a scavenger hunt; each find presenting another piece of a life raft. For Woody, the prospect of a stem cell solution was a point of focus—a monocular that, in part, filtered out the dark images shouting at him from all sides.

But there was a snag.

The religious right had the ear of President Bush. They'd essentially made an issue out of a non-issue, claiming that scientists were using embryos for futuristic experiments. Some even went so far as to accuse scientists of "killing unborn babies." What they didn't say was that, for the many years *before* embryonic stem cell research, in vitro clinics were simply destroying their unused embryos. What else *could* they do? There were hundreds of thousands of them, each about the size of a speck of dust, each filed away and kept refrigerated. It was that or store them indefinitely, *never* to be used. They certainly couldn't implant them to create babies, since the couples who owned them (and no longer needed them), didn't want them given out willy-nilly.

So it was a ridiculous argument, but an argument that Mr. Bush responded to.

It was a futile effort, I knew, but I wrote a letter to the president asking him to show the compassion he spoke of at the Republican Convention the year before. "Help my father and others like him. Please allow Federal Funding of Embryonic Stem Cell Research."

A few months later, I received a reply from the White House, dated July 2. Ironically, my dad's birthday. It was a form letter that Mr. Bush started by thanking me for my letter, then went on to say:

> I oppose Federal funding for stem-cell research that involves destroying living human embryos. I support innovative medical research on life-threatening and debilitating diseases, including promising research on stem cells from adult tissue.
>
> We have the technology to find these cures, and I want to make sure that the resources are available, as well. Only through a greater understanding, based on research, will we be able to find cures that will bring new hope and health to millions of Americans.
>
> Sincerely,
> George W. Bush

I never showed the letter to my dad, in part because he voted for Bush, and it would've felt like I was shoving my politics in his face. But more so because it was just another piece of bad news, and he'd had plenty.

The following month, the president issued a directive limiting federal research funding on embryonic stem cells to the sixty or so lines that were already available. Now research scientists, who were receiving federal funds, could no longer use any new lines of stem cells from frozen embryos.

After the president's directive, in vitro clinics across the country simply went back to destroying their unused embryos. It wasn't until March of 2009 that President Obama reversed the decision.

Still ALS has not yet been stopped, but there's hope.

With the president's stifling of federal funds, the bulk of the research would fall on private firms.

Actress Jenifer Estess was 35—the same age as Lou Gehrig—when she was diagnosed with ALS. In the aftermath of her diagnosis, she, along with her two sisters and friend Julianne Hoffenberg, founded Project ALS—a fund-raising venture to help pay for private research.

In the fall of 2001, I talked with Hoffenberg, and she was gracious enough to explain the progress of the research they were doing. She said the biggest obstacle they were facing was in *delivering* the stem cells to the afflicted motor neurons. They were making progress, she said, though slowly, incrementally. Still it was heartening, all of it. I passed along my best wishes to Jenifer Estess, who at such a young age, was facing down the most daunting of diseases. At the end of our conversation, Hoffenberg promised to pass me information as it became available to her.

A few weeks later, I was in my office taking a break from the rewrite room when I received an email from Hoffenberg about a new development. Her source was Jenifer's sister Valerie, who was with the ALS researchers in Maryland. Dr. Brian Kaspar (from the Salk Institute at La Jolla) and Dr. Jeffery Rothstein (from Johns Hopkins) had made something of a breakthrough. In their search for a viable delivery system, it seemed they'd found a viral vector (a tool commonly used by molecular biologists to deliver genetic material to cells) with real possibilities:

> What [the doctors] discovered a few months ago was that this particular viral vector, which…is benign (doesn't even cause as much as the flu), had the ability to travel "retrograde" to motor neurons. In other words, if injected into the muscle, the vector-plus-medicine could ride the monster roller coaster of the central nervous system backwards, from the injection site (the muscle), out to where the muscle and nerve speak to each other (the neuromuscular junction), up the winnowy motor axon, and, finally, into the motor neuron itself.

I didn't call my dad with the news, since conversations on the phone were difficult, but it was Tuesday, so I knew he'd be at *Becker's* filming that night. Then I could just show him the email.

As the audience was filing in, I found Woody in his usual front row seat, just behind the monitors. I stepped over to the railing with Hoffenberg's email, and handed it to him through the railing and across the walkway. He took it and looked at me quizzically. I told him it was from ALS researchers and to read the highlighted section. He read it as I watched. After a moment he looked at me with a quizzical look. I shrugged and said, "They're getting there, Dad. Who knows." He smiled and then started to cry. I walked past the side of the stage, past the guard and up to the audience where I made my way to him. I sat down on the carpeted step beside his seat and smiled up at him. "Pretty cool, huh?"

He ran his hand along my back and rested it on my far shoulder. He was still crying and drew a tissue from his pocket to wipe the tears from his eyes. He was happy.

As Robert Lee, the warm up guy, introduced himself to the audience, one of the writers on the stage, Kate, looked over and saw me sitting on the step next to Woody. And, as he rubbed my back and wiped the tears from his face, she mouthed a question to me. "Is he okay?"

I nodded and then my dad looked over and saw her concerned look. He smiled at her and shoved his thumb up in the air.

Ultimately, he could not be saved by stem cell research, restrictions by the Bush Administration or no. There wasn't the time. But that wasn't why I encouraged him to believe in it and even began to believe in it myself.

It was a tiny piece of hope. And hope, real or perceived, had value.

Though both he and Jenifer Estess would lose their hard-fought battles with ALS, hope was at least a weapon they could wield in the fight.

"It's like I have ESPN or something."
   Mean Girls

TEN
Visiting the Other Side

I had been through enough therapy to know that I wasn't supposed to assume what others were thinking or take on the emotions of others.

And I tried not to.

But as the effects of ALS took one ability after the next from my dad, I found it increasingly difficult not to worry about what he was thinking, and moreover what he was feeling. Neither was it something I felt comfortable asking him about since, like so many men of his generation, he was never one much for discussing his emotions. As well, his communication with me was limited to the LightWRITER, which hardly lent itself to in-depth explanations. So, more often than not, I found myself trying to gauge his sentiment by catching his expression in an off moment. And when it looked like the weight of the dark beast was crushing him, I felt my own heart being crushed.

In some ways, I felt worse for him *after* his life was filled with loved ones and friends because it was clear he was giving up so much more. He relished this new life, this new world, and I knew he wanted to remain in its warm embrace; I knew he wanted to continue this fantasy. But our fanciful hopes of a stem cell intervention were fading with the ineluctable plunge of the setting sun. I could see in his eyes the growing realization that he would not win this race, could not possibly, and that he would soon have to leave behind all that he had newly discovered and grown to love. I was drawn back to memories of my own darker days (in my mid-twenties), when it had occurred to me that life was frequently *most* cruel in the midst of a happy environment.

As things became increasingly difficult for him, I wanted *him* to believe there was more to this world than just what he saw. He was not, by any stretch, a religious man. I'd never heard him talk about God. When I was small, he donned a shirt and tie and went to church with my mother and me, because my mother was a devout Catholic—though later, she was more of an on-again-off-again Catholic. (She'd heard from someone that priests were having sex with nuns—so she was out. Then, perhaps ten years later, she asked a priest if it was true. He said no—so she was back in. *In hindsight, and in light of ongoing investigations, maybe she just wasn't being specific enough.*) But I don't think Woody ever took any religion seriously. In fact, I remember him referring to one of the churches my mother attended in the Bay Area (*The Most Sacred Blood*) as the "*Bucket of Blood.*" Out of my mother's earshot, of course.

And while I'd be hard-pressed to say that I ended up having a strong belief in any particular religion, I do believe there's *something*. Something that has created or orchestrated or manipulated the materials of this world we live in. Including us. There is some form of consciousness beyond the forms we live within. In that sense, I believe in God. And as I saw my father getting closer to death, I found it harder to accept that he had not even a fantasy about what came next. In truth I suppose I wanted to comfort myself by pointing out to him that there *might* be more past the doors of life than just a free-fall into nothingness.

Then I remembered something my aunt Oleta had told me several years earlier. It was a story about her mother, their mother, Arabelle, when she was dying of cancer in the summer of 1989. Oleta had moved to Sacramento to be with Arabelle during this period (as she would do later for Woody).

Now, it must first be pointed out that Arabelle, born in 1904, was pragmatic, no-nonsense, salt-of-the-earth. She was a Baptist, but in name only, who married young and for many years ran a diner in a small town on the flatlands of Texas. She was forthright and sensible, didn't tolerate bullshit (or infidelity for that matter, stepping ahead of her generation with the divorce of my grandfather in the 1940s). All of which is to say, she was not, by any stretch, a dabbler in the touchy-feely realm of the ethereal.

Near the end of her struggle with cancer, she slipped into unconsciousness for several hours. When she roused, she told my aunt what she'd seen while she was "away." It is a familiar story: There was a radiant white light, comforting in its embrace, and she was drawn toward it. When she approached the light, she found herself surrounded by a peaceful, loving feeling, a feeling of complete safety and well-being. As she walked farther into the light, she saw people she knew, people she loved, her mother, her father, a sibling; all of them having long since passed away. They beseeched her to join them. She said she was tempted to go, to be with them.

"Well, why didn't you?" Oleta asked her.

"I wanted to," Arabelle said. "But..."

"But what?"

Arabella looked up at her daughter. "But...who will take care of you?"

At the time Oleta was in her mid-sixties, had raised a family of her own, was in fact a great grandmother herself. She smiled and assured her mother that she was fully capable of taking care of herself. She said that if it was time for Arabelle to go, she could go.

Arabelle went to sleep that night and never woke.

My father was there, knew the story from Oleta, but I didn't know if it had any impact on him.

Before it became the soundstage for *Dr. Phil,* the soundstage next to *Becker's* was the soundstage for a pilot called *Oracles.* It was a "paranormal" show that delved into the afterlife, featuring a guy named Kenny King, who could, apparently, talk to the dead.

As I passed the *Oracle* sign in front of the stage each day, I started to formulate an idea. I wondered if maybe this guy, Kenny King, would talk to someone dead that Woody knew...if only to open Woody's mind to the possibility that—perhaps, maybe—there was more. I should point out, however, that I honestly don't know where I stand on the whole talking-to-the-dead thing, beyond entertainment. But that wasn't my point. Nor was it my objective when I got Kenny's number through a friend of mine.

His real name is Kenny Kynoch, a young guy. I asked him if he ever did private readings. Before I finished the question, he was assuring me he did indeed do such things, that, yes, yes, he'd be happy to.

When I saw my dad and my aunt that evening, I casually mentioned that I was thinking of doing something a little unusual. For fun. There was this guy, I explained, near where I work, who says he can talk to the dead. So I figured we could have him come by the house and, you know, talk to the dead. My dad was amused and didn't seem to give it a second thought as he typed out, "SURE." My aunt, as well, was fine with the idea.

I invited Gary Dontzig to join us. He being an intensely spiritual person, I figured he was an excellent candidate for the "séance," if that's what it was. He'd also lost a great many friends to AIDS during the 1980s. (This was before his partner Gary Campbell died.) In fact, during our early days at *Murphy Brown*, Dontzig would spend many of his mornings before work at a hospital, visiting a dying friend. And then, after work, after writing comedy all day, he'd spend his evenings sitting at the bedside of some other dying friend. That's who this guy is.

And I invited Jodi, my dad's "fan." Jodi and I had known each other since the early '80s, when we were both working at MTM. She had been, lately, spending a good deal of time with Oleta and Woody, dropping by in the afternoons, hanging around, watching TV; and they were, the three of them, becoming pretty chummy. So I figured, why not Jodi? Though I didn't know it when I invited her; she was an absolute non-believer in any-

and-all things airy-fairy hocus-pocus...like exactly what I had in mind.

He looked mostly uncomfortable as he stood in the dim glow of Woody's porch light. Kenny was in his early 20s with a baby face and dark, vulnerable eyes. His cheeks glowed red over mostly pasty skin, like he'd just come in from a blizzard or had sex. His jersey t-shirt hung loose over a large, awkward frame. It looked like he wasn't supposed to be heavy, but the weight just snuck up on him.

I stepped out onto the porch and closed the front door behind me, so I could pay him and speak privately.

"Oh, thank you," he said, when I gave him the cash. "Thanks a lot."

"Well, thanks for doing this. Really."

His next question threw me. "Listen," he said, "you don't know of anyone who's renting a room, do you?"

"A room? Well, no. Sorry."

"'Cause I'm living in my car now," he said, cringing a little, "and I gotta find a place to live, you know...just till they're finished shooting my pilot." It was a sentence one doesn't hear that often.

I thought about offering him the loft in our house... but reason and paternal responsibility clanged like a fire bell in my head. I didn't *know* him. And the house was where my family lived. Yes, he had a pilot, but he also talked to the dead. It flashed in my mind that we could *all* be dead by the morning. I told him I'd ask around.

After he was ushered in and introduced to everyone, he insisted that none of us tell him anything about ourselves. Nothing at all. Nothing. Then he sat on a chair in the middle of the TV room, while I sat next to my dad and Oleta. Gary and Jodi sat on either side of the room.

As we settled in and prepared for whatever was to come, I was secretly hoping my grandmother would show up—Arabelle. I'd always liked her. And certainly, with the three of us in the room, I figured it was a good bet she would.

My aunt volunteered to go first.

Kenny nodded, concentrated and then began to vigorously rub his upper thigh. Back and forth, back and forth, like he was scratching an itch. Hard. Rubbing, rubbing, rubbing. I was trying to figure out how the friction helped him get in touch with the dead or, if maybe, he'd just run across some poison oak. Whatever it was, it was odd...but then *he* was the professional, not me.

A moment later, after I suppose the appropriate amount of knuckle-leg rubbing, he said he was "getting something." "The letters 'I' and 'N'," he said. "Is there someone with the letters "IN" in their name?" (I've never really understood why dead people don't just come out and *tell* you their names, instead of this bullshit game of cat 'n' mouse. But again, not the professional.)

My aunt shrugged and surmised it might be her daughter, Linda, who had died only a few months earlier after a long battle with cancer. She was 53. Oleta was, of course, cautious, but nonetheless intrigued.

Kenny said Linda wanted to tell Oleta that she was fine, that she was finally at peace, and that she wanted Oleta to stop worrying about her. But, as Kenny was about to relay something more from Linda, he stopped.

He was getting a message from someone else. Someone who didn't seem to mind interrupting.

My mother.

Never mind that Linda had been talking. Never mind that Oleta was interested in what her daughter might have to say. Linda, however, had always been a thoughtful person, accommodating in life, and apparently now accommodating in death, as she agreed to step aside so that my mother could talk.

So, okay, while Kenny rubbed, rubbed, rubbed, I still hadn't quite bought into the whole thing. Nonetheless I found myself oddly irritated by what my mother was up to. If Kenny was gaming us, he sure had a pretty good sense of incorporeal personalities.

She, my mother, started by addressing my dad. Kenny rubbing, rubbing. She said she'd always felt he was kind. A kind man. And that she wasn't good enough for him.

Not altogether unlike her. In life, she was often conciliatory, frequently contrite. Which is, by the way, a familiar cycle in abusive relationships—this assault-apologize-assault-apologize dynamic. Often it is a symptom of the alcoholic personality, which was a part of the picture. But she was only this way with me. I'd never heard her apologize to my father. For anything.

Then Kenny turned to me. He was furiously rubbing his leg now. It was presumably still my mother and I was becoming uncomfortable. She was not yet dead a year, and frankly, I wasn't ready to deal with her again.

"She wants you to know..." Kenny said, looking at me, "that she's sorry she hurt you." With this, of course, I wanted to slip out of my skin and crawl away. It was always awkward when she apologized—interestingly, even after she was dead. "She says she knows she treated you badly, especially when you were in high school." That was certainly spot on. "But she says she always loved you."

I knew that was coming. It always did. The trouble was, I had long before learned that the words were thin, that they most often blew away with the next gust of wind. (Though, to be fair, in this instance, what gust of wind could that be?) And while I was feeling a rush of adolescent emotions, I was trying to remind myself that this could just be Kenny's bullshit.

When finally my mother relinquished Kenny back to Linda, most of what was said by Linda was general enough that Kenny could very well have been winging it. Though later, Oleta told me that "Linda" certainly sounded like her daughter, that Kenny's "Linda" said the sort of things Linda would say.

Then Kenny turned to Gary.

Rubbing, rubbing, rubbing.

And rubbing.

Finally...he said he had nothing.

There was no one on the other side who wanted to talk to Gary. It was peculiar. Of everyone who was sitting in that room, Gary was the one person who had a surfeit of friends "on the other side," friends who would have *wanted* to talk to him. Plus, he studied Eastern philosophies, practiced Tai Chi, he was a vegan, he was even friends with Marianne Williamson.

Still, Kenny was suspicious of Gary's intent; he thought Gary was "resisting" the process. Gary shook his head no, said he was completely, totally, receptive to talking to a deceased friend. Totally. *Any* deceased friend. Kenny gave his leg a few more good rubs, aggressive rubs. In fact, I was afraid he might draw blood. He was determined to get in touch with someone Gary knew. Finally...Kenny just gave up. He seemed vastly disappointed in Gary, certain I'm sure that Gary had done something wrong.

Kenny then turned to Jodi—the cynic, the nihilist. He started to rub his leg, said he sensed that she was putting up a block. Jodi said she wasn't blocking anything, she just thought that all of this was—in not so many words—a lotta crap. Kenny nodded, continued to rub his leg, and then asked her if there was someone in her life who loved horses. Jodi shook her head. No.

Gary, though, he knew someone. This person, Gary said, was someone he was very close to. This person *loved* horses.

Kenny shot him a look. "Not you." As he turned back to Jodi, rubbing, rubbing, rubbing. He said he was hearing from someone. A smirk from Jodi. Rubbing, rubbing. It was Jodi's mom—who had been dead about ten years. She and Jodi were very close, and I remember Jodi going though a long and painful period of mourning.

Jodi shifted in her seat. She was still a block of ice, but she was listening.

Kenny kept rubbing. "She wants to offer you proof."

"Proof?" Jodi said.

"She wants to offer you proof that it's her."

"Oh." Jodi's gaze narrowed. "Fine."

More rubbing.

"She wants to offer something about...a car. The car. Something you two shared. Just the two of you. In the car."

The chill in Jodi's demeanor was not thawing. "Uh-huh..." Clearly Jodi's mom and Kenny would have to come up with more than just a car.

"Your mother is telling me something..." A long pause, with rubbing. "A name. Roy. Does the name 'Roy' mean anything to you?"

"Roy?" she said, determined not to give away anything.

"Yes," Kenny said. "I keep getting the name Roy. Very strong. Very definitely Roy. Is that significant? You and your mother had a special thing about Roy. Your mother is offering this as proof."

While Jodi considered this, Kenny kept rubbing, "listening" for more.

As it turned out, "Roy" *did* mean something to Jodi. Roy had been the funny little secret she shared with her mom. When Jodi was in junior high, she had a major crush on a guy named Roy. He lived in another part of her town and, each morning, when her mom drove her to school, they took the long way, so that they could drive past Roy's house.

That was their thing.

I don't know how impressed Jodi was—I got the feeling that anything short of her mother climbing in through the window and throwing a plate across the room would not have impressed her

But *I* thought it was impressive.

As to my original objective, I don't know that any of it influenced Woody's view of a possible afterlife. It seems to me that he took all of it into consideration, and then just moved on with the living of his life. He was like that, and perhaps it is why he'd always been so untroubled by most of life's vicissitudes. It is how I think many of his generation were. "Yeah, yeah, it's all very interesting, but what is *is*."

ELEVEN
The Gala

He had no idea how to pin French cuffs.

I stepped over to him, picked up the oval cufflinks and put them in my mouth—the way he used to put spare nails in his mouth when he was building a fence. I folded the cuff, pinched the holes together, took a cufflink and ran the stud of it through them. As I moved to the other sleeve, I noticed his cummerbund. "We're gonna have to turn the cummerbund over, Dad. The little folds are supposed go upside down." He gave me a look 'cause, honestly, what did it matter? I shrugged. "Originally, the folds were supposed to catch bread crumbs." Which rendered it that much more pointless because he wouldn't be eating bread.

His fingers were losing their dexterity, so he handed me the clip-on tie. I straightened his collar and buttoned it so I could clip the tie in place. As I did, I remembered an evening some thirty or so years earlier: I was thirteen, standing in front of the bathroom mirror, growing more and more frustrated, tying, untying and retying one of my dad's neckties into a number of bizarre configurations—none of them resembling the tidy knot I saw each morning beneath my father's chin.

I'd asked an eighth grader, Sally Wilson—a year ahead of me—if she'd go to the dance on Friday, my first dance, my first date. To my joy and then mortification, she said yes.

As I stood in front of the bathroom mirror that Friday night, looking at the mangled knot at my neck like it was a growth, I felt like I was in over my head. Never mind any concerns about getting to "first base" (which, at 13, would've been, what, touching her hand—something I was too terrified to even attempt). Then there was the possibility of screwing up dance floor protocol, or that I might look like I had no idea how to dance—which I hadn't. And, of course, there was the *most* terrifying aspect of all—the Slow Dance. Not so much the dance itself, but the danger it presented of walking back to the boys' side of the gym with a boner.

Okay, so the tie.

I gave up on the ludicrous idea of unilaterally tying it and walked into the living room to ask my dad for help. He smiled, put the newspaper down, got up and walked me back into the bathroom where he stood me in front of the mirror and then moved behind me. He reached around to pull the wide end of the tie down below my belt. "You wanna give yourself plenty extra here," he said, then held the narrow end and flipped the wide end over, around, under and through its opening at the top, explaining as he went along. When he was finished, we both looked at me in the mirror. He smiled again and patted me on the shoulder. "Just takes a little practice is all."

When I finished clipping the tie to his tux shirt and clenched the bows on either side to straighten it, Oleta and Catherine admired our handiwork. "Very handsome," my aunt said, beaming at her brother. "Yes,"

Cath added, "very handsome."

My dad smiled and moved to the LightWRITER on the kitchen counter. He typed out a couple of words and then pushed the button. "THANK YOU."

"Okay, your limo should be here in half an hour," I said. "Cath and I gotta leave, 'cause we need to be there early."

Becker was being given an award that night by the Muscular Dystrophy Association. The MDA throws a high-priced bash each year to recognize certain media efforts that shed light on muscular dystrophy (ALS falls into this category since it affects the body's muscle groups).

When an organizer asked me if the *Becker* actors would be attending, I was not optimistic. I told him I'd ask but, frankly, since the event was scheduled for April (during the show's hiatus), the actors could very likely be just about anywhere in the world.

But, when I walked down to the stage to tell them about it, only two said they would be out of town. Terry Farrell and Saverio Guerra. The others—Ted, Hattie, Alex Desert (who played Jake, the blind newsstand guy at the diner) and Shawnee—said, if it's for Woody, they'd be there.

The ceremony was held at the Beverly Hilton, where red carpet flowed from the sidewalk over the hotel's opulent doorway and through the entry, where towering monoliths of glistening ice sparkled with streams of cascading vodka that flowed over frosted Russian logos. Fat black cameras dashed light around the room, whirring one after the next, as waiters floated through the milling penguins and sequined gowns, proffering hors d'oeuvre trays billowing with plump shrimp, bruschetta, stuffed mushrooms, truffle canapés. An opening to the side of the gallery led to a "media room," where press-like interviews were being video-taped under hot lights, and where guests squeezed themselves beside tolerant celebrities for their souvenir group shots and two-shots. Beyond the media room was the hotel's expansive dining room, where the Golden Globes are presented each year.

With his sister on his arm, Woody stepped from the entryway into the dining room and craned his neck to take in the massive chandeliers that swept across the ceiling like rivers of glass. Catherine and I joined them at a table on the main floor. Oleta slid into the seat beside her brother, where shimmering silver knives flanked elegant dinnerware. She looked up at the daffodils, lilies and daisies that shot up from the center of the table like a floral geyser and said, "Oh my."

Dinner arrived in waves, and I knew my dad had never seen an outlay of food like the one arriving at our table. Medallions of beef under a medley of savory sauces beside tender shoots of buttery asparagus and carrot timbale, followed by flared structures of white and dark chocolate, dripping with dark raspberry sauce. Which, again, he couldn't eat. He could smell it. He could long for it. But he couldn't eat it. By this point, he could no longer chew and swallow anything solid, though he could still eat soups and finely pureed vegetables and fruits. So I asked one of the waiters if he could help us out, find some soup in the kitchen, anything, but he seemed flummoxed by the request. They had food for everyone but the guest of honor?

My dad poked my arm, and showed me the LightWRITER: "IT'S OKAY."

"No," I said. "They gotta have something you can eat here, Dad. Good God, you're one of Jerry's Kids!" I got up and crossed for the double doors of the kitchen to navigate the labyrinthine recesses of its stainless steel maze, looking for signs of life. Eventually I found someone, a small Hispanic man who was very confused by my appearance there, but he agreed to scare up some tomato soup and bring it out to us.

When I made my way back to the table, I saw that Ted had taken my seat. He was laughing at something Woody was typing on the computer. Since my seat was taken, I wandered over to the neighboring table where the actors were seated. I plopped down in an empty seat next to Alex, and nodded toward Ted. "Sonofabitch over there stars in a few sitcoms, thinks he can sit anywhere he wants."

Alex glanced at the table. "Yeah, he's an asshole."

As we chatted, I kept an eye on the other table. My dad and Ted were passing the LightWRITER back and forth, laughing at whatever one or the other had typed out. And then, a couple of times, Ted just leaned over and hugged Woody.

That he showed so much attention and affection to my dad was a joy to watch. For Woody's part, I think he was partially amazed to have developed a friendship with Ted Danson. He and my mother watched *Cheers* regularly through the '80s, and I'm sure my dad never expected to even *meet* the star. Beyond that, beyond all the Sam Malone stuff, Woody truly appreciated the sincerity of Ted's affection and the friendship itself.

Casey Kasem was hosting the evening's presentation, and when he introduced himself by doing an impression of *Scooby-Doo's* Shaggy, Ted hugged my dad again, got up and moved back to his own seat. As I sidled back into mine, I could see my dad was having a great time. My aunt then leaned across to me and said to look at what Ted had just typed into the machine. The screen showed, "YOU AND YOUR SO." I pressed a button and the words scrolled: "YOU AND YOUR SON HAVE MADE THIS YEAR A VERY SWEET AND TENDER YEAR FOR ME, AND I HAVE FALLEN IN LOVE WITH YOUR SON. HE IS A SWEET SOUL."

TWELVE
Big Bear

I missed the crisp air of Lake Tahoe; the way it filled the senses like a brisk slap in the face. I missed the neon blue sky, forever framed—like the cobalt water of the lake beneath it—by soaring Douglas-fir and Ponderosa Pines. Where early in the morning you could hear an outboard motor sputter to life across the lake and a man's voice crack along the water's surface just up the shore. Where a fish bursts through the glassy water's top and splashes back down like an iced tea commercial.

Having spent high school in Fair Oaks, near Sacramento, and college in Chico, farther upstate—both an hour or two away from Tahoe—I'd been up to the lake a number of times and came to relish my time there. So when I found out that Catherine's parents would be visiting in the summer, I thought Tahoe would be a great place to go for the Memorial Day weekend. But it was more than a stone's throw from Los Angeles, and getting everybody there—us, the boys, Cath's parents, Woody and Oleta—looked like preparing for an Allied invasion. After my slew of hyperbolic complaints about organizing such a sojourn, Cath came up with a getaway compromise that promised a similar blue sky over a sparkling lake, with green pines, at a fraction of the distance: Big Bear.

Her parents were spending about six weeks with us which, when I mentioned as much to friends, the news was generally met with polite expressions of sympathy. But the truth was—and this will sound odd—I enjoyed the company of my in-laws. No, I'm serious. They seemed to know how to stay in someone's home and become a functioning part, an independent part, a welcome presence, instead of a nuisance or an obligation. Kevin, in his mid-seventies, and Mary, in her mid-sixties, were used to traveling, often with groups of friends, forever learning, reading, meeting new people, always curious. Devout and steadfast Catholics, their only requirement was the address of the nearest Catholic church and the times of its Sunday Masses.

Generally, Australians are much more familiar with extended travel than Americans. If you think about it, as soon as an Aussie leaves Australia, there's no way to take a *short* trip. Once the plane has lifted off, it makes no sense to fly 14 or 16 hours, then turn around and come back in a few days. So when Australians travel, they're generally gone for many weeks or months. To that end, young people in Australia, after they've finished college, often take a year or two to travel, *just* travel. And when they return, their applications for work include a reference to having done so. As a point of pride. Admirably, that experience is welcomed by Australian employers.

Cath, with her parents and Joe, drove up to Big Bear on Friday morning of the Memorial Day weekend. I stayed in L.A. until Henry was finished with school later that afternoon, then we drove up to meet them. Oleta and my dad were driving up on Saturday.

The cabin we'd rented was nestled amidst the requisite pines on the side of a mountain, just up the street from the lake. Spacious inside, there were three bedrooms upstairs; kitchen, living room downstairs, a massive rock fireplace faced by a sweeping earth-tone burlapy-ish couch. The place was a little retro, funky even, with its wood paneling, green shag carpet and a stereo system from an ad in a '70s Playboy.

No matter, the scent of fresh pine was thick, the sky was cerulean—it was the perfect fill-in for Tahoe. The perfect set up, for what would turn out to be a shit weekend.

On our first night, before Woody and Oleta arrived, we piled into the Jeep and went looking for a Mexican restaurant. The town itself was small; bait and tackle shops, a palm reader, boat sales, Realtors and a McDonald's. We managed to find a Mexican restaurant and gorged ourselves before returning to the cabin, where I was looking forward to a game of cards or *Backgammon* or *Monopoly*, since the cabin came with a ready supply of games.

Unfortunately, Joe brought along a game that was his obsession at the time—*Yu-Gi-Oh!*—and, even more unfortunately, he managed to coerce me into playing. The game is a series of cards with pictures of colorful monsters and heroes and various personalities that are dealt out, flipped over, moved around and collected with, what appeared to me, no rhyme or reason.

So, Joe—not quite five at the time—sat me down and dealt out a series of cards, explaining with some authority what each could do, its value and when it should or should not be used. Nothing of what he was telling me made any sense, so I picked up the instruction book, while he finished dealing out the deck. From what I could discern (pay close attention): The Shield & Sword card, when activated, excluded any summoned Monsters, while the Star Boy card had an Aqua/Effect as long as it was face-up, which increased the ATK of all Water Monsters by 500 points. The Scapegoat Card, when activated, could *not* summon any Monster in the same turn, including Flip Summon and Special Summon; and the Sheep Token couldn't be used as a Tribute for a Tribute Summon. All of this seemed to make complete sense to Joe (while I had an eerie sense that I was back in the high school physiology class I flunked out of, after staring blankly at a final exam I hadn't prepare for).

Joe was shifting cards and flipping others like a fry cook, and each time I asked a question, I was met with a weighted sigh and then an explanation I didn't understand. Near the end of the game—or the middle or the beginning, I don't know—Henry sat down with some ice cream to watch us. Confident now that I had an impartial six-year-old witness to the veritable rabbit's hole I'd been conned into, I turned to him (after losing a Water Monster to an ATK) and asked if it made sense to him. Surely, he'd back me up on this Kafka-esque mindfuck. He studied the cards for a moment and said, "You're lucky the ATK didn't take *all* of your Water Monsters. "

Saturday morning, the weather was beautiful.

It was sunny.

Pancakes, bacon, eggs greeted even the late risers (Henry and Joe). It was the perfect mountain cabin breakfast. (These two, especially Henry, never got out of bed before ten or eleven. Believe it or not, Henry would sleep late on *Christmas*. Something that made me doubt I'd ever be able to relate to this kid.)

In the early afternoon, Henry, Joe and I were headed out to do some exploring along the mountainside. Oleta and my dad arrived just as we were about to start our adventure. We said hi, and I showed them into the cabin. Though I didn't put any particular import to it, my dad seemed subdued, like he was there, but he didn't really want to be. It wasn't like him. I thought maybe after he relaxed, maybe after he took a nap, he'd feel better.

Whatever, the boys and I were off for parts unknown.

On the way up the initial slope, we discussed with anticipation all of the creatures we might encounter along the way. Bugs, of course, plenty of bugs. Lizards certainly. Maybe we'd even *catch* a few lizards to bring back and show everybody. *That*, I thought, would be entertaining. I was sure there'd be squirrels, maybe even a skunk or a porcupine, a raccoon, a deer? An eagle? As we climbed higher, so did Joe and Henry's conjectures. Maybe we'd see a bear or a mountain lion. Right, Joe agreed, or an orangutan. Or a herd of el-phants—Henry. As we stepped aside for some mountain bikers, I tried to temper the boys' expectations, pointing out that it was fairly unlikely we'd run across any orangutans or elephants. They were a little annoyed with me for dashing cold water on their aspirations.

Their disappointment and annoyance soon gave way to delight though as we made our way up the face of the mountain and discovered rock formations they were sure no human had ever before set eyes on. Henry, however, always the circumspect one, the cautious one, was growing concerned about finding our way back to the cabin. I told him not to worry, that I had been bending the odd branch to mark our way.

One of the more interesting junctures of our journey happened as we faced a precarious path along the slope of a monolithic rock with a near sheer drop of maybe twenty feet. A little scary, yes, but I told the boys that it's okay to be afraid, just concentrate on the other side, trust yourself and move ahead. It was a quintessential fathery moment—eliciting within the male parent the instinct to teach his sons the acknowledgement of fear and the need to work past it. It is the same paternal drive that makes a father transform the snarl of a dog, a bully's threat or a bruised knee into the cornerstone of a future American statesman. Confidence in the face of (perceived) danger—what more valuable a lesson could there be?

We each studied the narrow path for a moment, and then made our way across it, slowly, cautiously, one step at a time, arriving on the other side without a single loss of life.

Admittedly, this is one of the more annoying traits that fatherhood had instilled in me—the quest to find "life lessons" at every turn. My father imparted many to me, though it seems the smaller of them were the ones that stood out. Like the time at our dinner table when I was eight and couldn't fathom the thought of eating the disgusting pile of green peas on my plate. My disdain was probably obvious and, when my mother went back into the kitchen, my dad leaned over and quietly taught me how to mesh some of the peas in the middle with my fork, then push them out to the sides, so as to create a hole. "See there," he said, showing me his own plate. "Makes it look like you've eaten a lot of 'em."

When I was 12, my mother found a copy of Playboy hidden in my bedroom. A classic scenario, to be sure. She was livid and obviously told my dad. So he came into my room, closed the door, found the magazine and sat down with me. As he flipped through it, he said, "You know, Rusty, a lot of boobs don't really look like that." He handed it back to me, told me to find a better hiding place, got up and left.

Then there was the time I'd screwed up something in high school—what it was I've now long forgotten. I was sitting on my bed when my dad rapped lightly on the door to my room, walked in and sat down beside me. He knew I was upset and, after a moment, he put a hand on my shoulder and said, "Ya know, Russell T., when you head into the clubhouse after a round of golf, the trick is to forget about the shots you missed. Remember the ones you made."

After the boys and I met and conquered our mountainside challenges, we headed back down to the cabin. Unfortunately, we hadn't seen any of the creatures we'd envisioned. Well, two lizards. When we did, Henry and Joe were so overcome that they screamed and chased after them. Which, I had to point out, was not the best way to catch lizards.

Another life lesson.

When we returned from the wilderness, we walked into the living room of the cabin like Odysseus & Sons.

Catherine and her parents had gone out shopping. Oleta was in the kitchen and my dad was sitting quietly on the couch, not watching TV, not doing anything but sitting. My aunt looked at me, concerned, and motioned that she and I step outside.

"I think he's having trouble breathing," she said. "The air up here. It's too thin. It's too hard on his lungs. The muscles around his lungs."

"Oh my God," I said. "Shit. I didn't even think of that."

"I didn't think of it either," she said, shaking her head and looking back towards the cabin.

"Wull, what did he say? Did he say anything?"

"He's trying to act like everything's okay. He keeps saying he's okay." She bit her lower lip, and looked momentarily back at the cabin. Then she turned back to me. "But I don't think he is."

"Goddamnit! Goddamnit!" I said, and then headed back into the cabin.

I saw him take a breath as I came into the room and then sat next to him on the couch. He looked tired, his thinning hands resting on top of the LightWRITER. I put a hand on his and asked if he was having trouble breathing. He looked at me and forced a half-hearted smile. Then he typed out, "A LITTLE."

"The air up here, I didn't even think of that."

He shrugged.

"Look, Dad, we'll pack up. You and me. And we'll head back. It's no sweat," I said, and then waited for him to type something.

"DON'T WANT TO RUIN YOUR WEEKEND."

I nearly laughed, it was so absurd. He couldn't

breathe, and he was concerned about ruining my weekend. "Dad, we're gonna load up and go."

Catherine and her parents were returning from the store, so I went out to meet them on the walkway. I didn't want to have the discussion in front of my dad. I was on the verge of tears when I told them, "Woody's having trouble breathing. I'm taking him back." Mary sighed sympathetically and Kevin nodded. Cath was looking at me as I turned abruptly and went back inside to head upstairs.

We had been having problems, Catherine and I, over the past few months. I had been spreading myself too thin. Admittedly, the spouse of a sitcom writer frequently grapples with the long and indeterminate hours that consume their mates. But my juggling those hours along with the time I was spending with my dad was taking its toll on us. And she had been expecting to use this time at Big Bear to talk some of it out—which she explained as she stepped into the bedroom where I was gathering my things.

Obviously, with the semi-emergency at hand, we wouldn't be able to discuss our problems, so she wanted to know when we would. And there, with a house full of relatives, we ended up arguing, all of course in hushed tones behind a closed door, but as hostile as we'd ever been with each other. To the point it implied, for both of us, the possible dissolution of the marriage.

A few moments later, everyone walked out to the car with my father and me. The driveway's gravel crunched like broken teeth beneath our feet, as the tension between Cath and me was palpable.

I threw our bags in the car and turned to say good-bye. Awkwardly I embraced Mary and Kevin and Oleta. I picked up and kissed Henry and then Joey. And then only said good-bye to Catherine.

As Woody and I drove away, I wanted desperately to let him know that he wasn't the cause of any of this, of the problems Cath and I were having. In my futile quest to protect him from as many things as I could, it pained me to think he might now be worrying about that too.

Besides, he loved Cath, adored her.

As we descended the mountain, Woody began to breathe more freely and started feeling better. So I figured I'd broach the subject. "You know," I said, affecting as much an air of casual as possible, "Cath and I have been having some problems."

He started typing something. I waited.

"BECAUSE OF ME."

There it was. It burned like a hot iron. In our reversed roles, the child was blaming himself for the parents' troubles. I couldn't bear his feeling responsible for any of it. And, honestly, he was a complication, not a cause. "No," I said, "she doesn't think I should be working so many hours." Which wasn't untrue.

We drove for another moment or two, and then I tried to lighten the moment. "Not sure if you realize this, Dad...but sometimes marriage is a lot of work."

He smiled appreciatively, thought about it a moment and then started typing. When he finished, he pushed the button on the machine. It said, "YOU GOT IT EASY."

"Tho' much is taken, much abides; and tho'
We are not now that strength which in old days
Moved earth and heaven; that which we are, we are;
One equal temper of heroic hearts,
Made weak by time and fate, but strong in will
To strive, to seek, to find, and not to yield."

             Ulysses, Alfred Lord Tennyson

THIRTEEN
The Things That Mattered

He was a man floating across the summer sky in a lawn chair, suspended beneath a bouquet of helium-filled balloons, each bursting, one by one.

By one.

While his voice slowly faded away over several months—as did his ability to swallow solid foods and then even liquids—the muscles that held his head upright seemed to fail him overnight. Without the aid of a padded neck brace, he was no longer afforded the dignity even of holding his head up. When he could no longer breathe while lying down, he was given a "bipap machine" that would pump air into his lungs while he slept. And, as his throat muscles became useless, his ability to dislodge phlegm vanished as well, requiring another machine, this one to suction out the sputum.

But still, it was the more trivial things that became most significant. The pedestrian, the workaday functions that, when healthy, we notice only barely in our periphery, like the familiar buildings we pass each day along the road.

For Woody, changing the physical world was key to his happiness and fuel for his survival. Constructing, repairing, adjusting, fixing things. Working with what existed. Building with hammer and nail, replacing a carburetor, connecting wooden stud to wooden stud with bolt and nut or surrounding a lawn with a new fence. When his ability to do so started to elude him, so too did much of his momentum.

It was a Saturday when he saw his dexterity slip away.

Catherine and I had taken Woody and the boys to *The Good Guys* (an electronics store) to find a new cabinet for his stereo system. And we found the perfect one—black wood on wheels, a glass front—that, unassembled in a box, took a great deal of effort by two bouncer-sized "Good Guys" in stretched black polo shirts, just to get it out to the parking lot and into the back of the SUV. Amusingly, it would be up to me *alone* to reverse the process when we returned to Woody's house.

After I backed the Jeep into the driveway, Catherine and the boys piled out and wandered off to various parts of the house, while Woody headed to the garage to get some tools for the cabinet's assembly.

I slid the box out the back of the SUV and slowly lowered it to the driveway, careful to bend at the knees. "Use your knees, not your back. Lift with your knees." It had forever been my dad's mantra when I was a kid.

This though, this was not just heavy, this was a cardboard-covered monolith from Stonehenge. As I struggled up the brick walkway with it, straining, sweating, groaning, half dragging it...I became the squirrel from *Ice Age*, teeth bared, grunting, eyes bulging like eggs.

About halfway up the walk, Joe of course jumped in to help...which slowed even further an already slow process. I did my best to involve him without ending up with a squished five-year-old. When finally it had been wrestled into the TV room, the plastic straps cut from it, the cardboard pried open to reveal its flat, lifeless black contents, I sat, sweating, breathing, feeling a headache coming on.

Putting it together though was going to be fun.

Woody met me in the TV room after returning from the garage. The array of tools out there was extensive. There was an air compressor with hydraulic attachments that could zip lug nuts off a wheel with a half-second of *vrrrreeeee-vrrreeeeee!* There were pipe wrenches and vice grips and electrical testers, a variety of saws, both electrical and manual; there was every tool imaginable, including some that looked like they might be used for enhanced interrogation.

Woody was carrying a rugged black and yellow case with a handle, built like the type used in military operations. He undid the latches and opened it to reveal a De-Walt battery-powered drill. This was *not* the sort of power drill you find in the pantry between a pink-handled hammer and a stack of *In Style* magazines. This was Black Ops grade, no-nonsense, war-ready weaponry. At its base—a solid black detachable battery pack that slammed up into the gun handle like a fully packed ammo clip.

I'd seen it a couple of times before—once when I was trying to tighten a troublesome screw on the slot car table with a conventional Phillips screwdriver. After struggling to drive the screw about halfway in, I felt Woody's hand on my shoulder, turned and saw the De-Walt driver. He motioned for me to step aside. Then he dropped the nose of the bit into the screw's star and *ziiip*, it was done.

While Woody, Joe and I sorted out the pieces of the cabinet on the floor of the TV room, Catherine was in the kitchen doing something, Henry in the backyard playing with the dog. After deciphering the Korean-written English instructions—"Place Section D until best side of Section C."—and then tracking down a few spare pieces that Joe had wandered off with, we were ready to assemble.

As I held Section D and C together, Woody got down on one knee and drove a series of screws into them. But the DeWalt was slowing down—the battery clip needed to be changed out. I picked up Section B, while my dad gripped the clip on either side of the driver's base and pinched it to pull the dying battery pack out. But he couldn't pinch hard enough to unlatch it. He grimaced as he tried again, squeezing, pushing his digits to perform the impossible. But there wasn't the strength. He couldn't apply the pressure.

In my youth, I'd seen him swing a ten-foot industrial pipe into place and hold it there with one hand, while he dropped a welder's mask over his face with his other hand, and then weld the pipe into place. Now he was looking at the DeWalt like a kid discovering his ruined baseball mitt. I was sitting on the floor amidst the various cabinet pieces. He turned to me, a man falling away into an abyss. Tears welling in his eyes. He studied me a moment as though it was all a bad dream, one that I might wake him from.

But I couldn't.

Finally, he looked at the DeWalt and then dropped it to the floor. He clutched the side of his desk, stood slowly and wiped the dampness from his face. Then he walked to the den, putting a hand on the wall to make the step up. I got to my feet and watched him as he moved quietly through the unlit living room, past the slot car track and through the foyer into his bedroom, where he gently shut the door.

I'd never seen him give up on anything. Ever. He'd always found a way to make things work. A wobbly wheel could always be realigned or re-bent or salvaged for parts. A broken light fixture could be rerouted, re-worked, reshaped into working condition or used for something else. His garage was littered with parts, pieces of things, useless for their original intent, but vital to the improvised repair of a space heater or a coffee maker or a busted doggie door.

Working with his hands had sustained him. Not only around the house in Studio City, but through the many years of his marriage. As long as he could go out into the yard and work on a sprinkler system, or into the garage to rebuild a car's engine, he was happy.

Now even that was gone.

All that was left...was us.

He could still work the computer, but for a time seemed interested only in solitaire. There were movies we could watch.

There was that.

Going out to the movies, though, presented problems as his legs grew weaker. We eventually worked out a system at the Galleria—a mammoth movie complex in Sherman Oaks—whereby we'd pull into the valet service at the lower level of the mall, he'd walk the twenty or thirty feet to the elevator and take it to the theatres on the fourth floor. Meanwhile, I'd take the escalator to the third floor to buy tickets and then pop up to meet him on the fourth floor outside the theater's entrance.

Though things were getting tougher for him, there were still reasons to laugh, and he provided them. Coming back from the theater one day, I pulled out of the Galleria and saw that Ventura Boulevard was congested. I did a quick u-turn and explained to Woody that it was stupid to try to battle traffic on the boulevard when we could jump on the freeway and, bam, we'd be home in a shake. I was showing off a little as I zipped between a few slow-moving cars on Sepulveda Boulevard and darted for the freeway on-ramp. But as I turned the corner to enter the 101, bam, traffic was jammed as far as the eye could see. And not *slow-moving* jammed—it was cars and trucks and busses at a standstill.

I punched the steering wheel in frustration, and then heard Woody typing something. He looked up from the machine and grinned at me as he pressed the button. "SMOOOOTH."

Woody and I had haircuts scheduled in the afternoon.

Tom had been my barber for maybe 20 years. He was an affable guy, a few years older than I, who made jokes about being the only heterosexual "hair stylist" in

Los Angeles. He always had a dirty joke to pass on to Woody and a ready critique of whatever Woody was wearing that didn't match. My dad enjoyed him immensely. It was one more way that Woody had melded into my life, my world. (Woody, by the way, at 77, showed no signs of a receding hairline.)

Tom worked at a shop in the famous Brentwood Country Mart, near Santa Monica. A bit of a schlep from Studio City, but the Mart was fun. Painted red with white trim, from the street it looked a little like an old barn, while inside it looked a little like the corridors of a horse stable. It was the kind of place you'd see Rob Reiner under a baseball cap getting chicken, or Morgan Fairchild in sweats with a smoothie. And back in the day, O.J. Simpson in a mask with a knife (that last was a joke).

Joe and Henry liked to go with us because there was a toy store across the courtyard from the barbershop, and Grampa was always an easy touch. Then, after the toy store and haircuts, they usually scored something unhealthy and coveted from the snack counter in the courtyard near the fire pit.

We were running late, as usual, and hadn't left the house yet. I was sitting in the idle car with Henry, the car door still open. Woody was in the house rounding up Joe. Getting both boys into the car at the same time was like playing a game of whack-a-mole.

But it was taking Woody an especially long time, and I was about to go in to find Joe myself. Suddenly then, Joe burst out of the house, near tears, and came running to the car. "It's Grampa!" he yelled, and grabbed my hand to pull me out of the car and toward the house.

"What's wrong, Joe?" I said, as we ran up the walkway

to the front door.

"He was helping me tie my shoe. He helped me tie my shoe. He bent down, but now he can't get up!"

I stepped through the front door and saw Woody in the entryway, down on one knee, clinging to the doorknob of the coat closet. He was struggling, straining, to pull himself up, but he couldn't do it. He was too weak to lift his weight. All he could do was grip the doorknob and wait for help.

As I reached down and ran my hand under his arm, Joe was crying, trying to help me lift his grandfather to his feet. "I'm sorry, Grampa. I'm sorry," he said, as though he himself had crippled Woody.

"Joe, it's not your fault..." I said, as Henry showed up to see what was going on.

"I wanted Grampa to tie my shoe," Joe went on explaining, as he held his grandfather's hand, "'cause I couldn't tie my shoe, and I wanted Grampa to tie it for me, and then he couldn't get up, and I tried to help him get up, but I couldn't help..."

"Joe," I said, when Woody was standing on his own, "it's not your fault. Grampa's having problems with his muscles, that's all. It's okay. It isn't your fault. Really."

Meanwhile Woody had found the LightWRITER and typed, "IT'S OKAY, JOE."

As we walked back out to the car, Joe appeared at Woody's side and took hold of his hand. He wasn't about to let anything else happen to Grampa.

On the ride to Brentwood, Henry and Joe were uncharacteristically quiet in the back seat, each perhaps aware that Woody's predicament in the entryway of the house meant something more significant than a delay in our trip. My dad looked out the window, deep in thought. I reached over and put a hand on his leg. He laid his hand on top of mine. The traffic on the 405 sucked, and I made some lame joke about it.

The rest of the drive was quiet.

Meanwhile, I was trying to figure out what this would mean—in practical terms. What would have to change? Would he soon need a wheelchair? If so, would he be able to maneuver it with his hands, his arms, or would it have to be controlled by a motor and joystick? And, if he needed a wheelchair, adjustments will have to be made to the house, the yard, the car. What else?

For Woody, it was more than a harbinger of death— it was literal incremental death. His body was going away one piece at a time, balloon by balloon, while his mind—healthy as ever—was being held hostage, cruelly, within its moribund vessel.

Around him he'd discovered a new life, a new family, brimming with laughter and kind regard, its incipient form promising a future that he knew he'd never see. He wanted desperately to remain, to enjoy this new life, but the rest of him was leaving.

When I mentioned to my aunt on the phone that night what had happened, she sighed a sigh from deep within. "Well, I think it's time for me to move out to Studio City," she said.

In the time he had left, he would not need a wheelchair. The muscles around his lungs were deteriorating too quickly for that.

Still, there were surprises to come.

FOURTEEN
Options

"Rusty? You know how a horse eats corn?"

"No! No, I know, Daddy! I know! I already know!" I
screamed as I clambered across the bench seat toward
the passenger door. His right arm would then reach
over and wrap his massive fist around the flesh of my
leg just above the knee, where his fingers and thumb
tightened like an industrial clamp—the power of which
was indomitable. And while I squirmed, breathless from
laughter, pleading for mercy, he'd casually navigate the
narrow winding streets of the Oakland hills near our
house. An early form of multi-tasking, I suppose. Then
he'd take his hand back and put it on the steering wheel,
while he shifted his other arm to rest an elbow out the
opened window. "*That's* how a horse eats corn," he'd
say.

A few weeks before he died, when he and I were watching TV one night with Oleta, he looked over at me and
nodded cryptically at his right hand, while he raised it
slightly and quietly pinched the open air a few times. I
looked at him, not understanding. He glanced over at
his sister to be sure she was not paying attention, then
he typed out, "WAITED TOO LONG. NOT STRONG
ENOUGH." But he didn't press the button to make the

machine say the words out loud. I looked at him and nodded, though I wasn't sure exactly what he meant. Still, I had an eerie feeling it was darkly significant.

He struggled to get up out of his chair, picked up the LightWRITER, and waved for me to follow him. We walked into his bedroom, where he closed the door and then took me into the closet. He pointed to a shoebox on the shelf above his hanging clothes, so I pulled the box down and followed him back into the room to sit on the bed. I took the lid off the box and lifted the layer of tissue to find a camouflage pouch that unzipped to reveal a hand gun.

"You were gonna use this?"

He nodded. Then he typed out, "NOT NOW."

He wanted me to take the gun. To do something with it, so that it was not discovered amongst his things. I put it back in the pouch, the pouch back in the box and I said I'd take care of it.

He bought the gun a few years earlier, after he'd learned that his friend from the Marine Corps, Bill Willekie, used a gun to kill himself after being told he would have to live in a nursing home. That had always been a big thing for my dad, the idea of a nursing home. In fact, it was the one thing, the only thing, he ever asked of me throughout all of this. He made me promise never to put him in a nursing home.

He didn't seem to want to go into much detail about his own decision regarding the gun, so I didn't press.

Later, as I was leaving for the night, Oleta walked me to the front door. I stopped at the coat closet and opened it to take the shoebox from where I'd put it. "You don't know about this, do you?" I said quietly to her. "About what's in here?"

She looked at it and guessed, "Shoes?"

I shook my head, implying she was way off. She studied it for another moment and then just seemed to sense what I was getting at. She sighed and looked up at me.

I said good-night, kissed her and went home.

We left it at that.

Statistically speaking, ALS victims are 25 times more likely to die by suicide than people with other diseases, according to Dr. Linda Ganzini at Oregon Health and Science University.

I wasn't shocked to learn that my dad had planned to take his own life. And, having struggled with depression in my life, it was not an option I was unfamiliar with. In fact, it was something that Woody had saved me from many years earlier. He, of course, knew of my struggles with depression, but didn't know the rest. Didn't know how close I'd actually come to suicide in my early twenties (before I was treated with medication).

It dogged me, depression, on and off for a year and a half during college, nearly crippling me at times. And then after college it struck again and *did* cripple me as it bore down without respite for just over five months.

A black acid had consumed me. Every minute of each day was agony. The only relief came with the unconsciousness of sleep. Then, in those hazy seconds between oblivion and cognizance, all of it, all of the pain, would come rushing back in. And the moments afterward, as I lie in bed, awake and burning inside, ten minutes stretched out like an eternity. And when they had passed, those ten minutes, I could not fathom, for any price, ever going though them again. And yet, as I looked out at the day ahead of me, at the long stretch of consciousness to come, it was an endless string of ten-minute stretches, one after the next after the next after the next. "The pain," William Styron wrote in *Darkness Visible,* "is unrelenting, and what makes the condition intolerable is the foreknowledge that no remedy will come—not in a day, an hour, a month or a minute."

It is why I view the suicide of a depressed person not as "the easy way out," but as a final tragic, ineluctable and ultimately courageous leap. As well, it's why I rankle at the armchair quarterback who has not experienced clinical depression, yet opines from afar that suicide is a cowardly alternative to hardship. He is the illiterate bumpkin condemning the distinguished academic, the silver-spooned heir espousing frugality to the homeless. He doesn't know the depths of depression's dark anguish, nor its sinister tenacity; forcing, with its iron grip, the victim's every thought through a shadowed and dank tunnel; he makes assumptions from above the fray, but hasn't viewed the underside of depression's sludge-covered belly; he cannot comprehend all existence in the negative; an excruciating existence with no end, where there is no escape, no release from its scalding and relentless torment. What he doesn't understand is that the sufferer finally has no choice but to do the unspeakable, to destroy the center of their universe, to obliterate the self. It is an overwhelming decision, suicide; the *consequence* of a disease. Suicide is, after all, the loss of all love, the loss of all beauty. It is many horrible things. But it is not "the easy way out."

At the end of those five-plus months in my early

twenties, I was busing tables in a restaurant in Los Angeles, and doing a piss-poor job of it. When, at a certain point, I couldn't remember where the table was that I'd just stripped, I stood frozen in the middle of the dining room, fresh napkins and clean silverware in hand—and I broke. I just broke. I could not go on. A waitress stepped over and asked if I was okay. I could only stutter.

The restaurant manager took me to his office, checked the information page that I filled out when I took the job (I couldn't remember my home phone number) and called my parents in Sacramento. Later, with the help of my then girlfriend Laurie, I was booked on a flight up to Sacramento. When my dad picked me up at the airport, he reached down and took my bag, then he put his other arm around me and said, "Don't worry, kiddo. We'll figure this out."

It is what I had always appreciated about him; his ability to see beyond his own life experiences. Especially when it came to me. I don't think he had ever experienced a depressed day. As well, he was from a different generation, one that saw emotional illness as a freakish disease, something not spoken of. His was the pull-your-self-up-by-the-bootstraps generation, the can-do Greatest Generation. Yet here he was with an emotionally broken kid, damaged goods returned home, taken down by some vaporous unseen bugaboo.

He took me to see a psychiatrist the next day, and I was immediately prescribed anti-depressants. The doctor said though not to expect anything for a number of weeks. If there wasn't a lift in the symptoms by then, he said, he'd switch me to another medication.

Three weeks later, to the day, I took a deep breath

and felt like I could resume my life. Indeed it was a watershed moment, the gateway to a different life, one with a diminished threat of depression's anguish. And, with the torment held in reasonable abeyance, there came a certain freedom to make choices.

I am one of the lucky ones, having responded to the first medication I was given. Many do not, often having to go through the painful process of trial and error to find an effective medication. They must wait patiently while an impatient disease strangles them, and if the next medication doesn't work, they must move on to the next and the next. And for those who get to the end of the line, their only hope is electroconvulsive treatment, commonly referred to as electroshock. ECT is an extremely effective treatment for severe depression, though it's gotten a bad rap over the years, especially since *One Flew Over the Cuckoo's Nest*. The treatment resembles nothing of the exaggerated ordeal Nicholson went through, the procedure having been greatly refined and now administered under a general anesthetic. Still, it is not a cure. It does not guarantee immunity, but it is a barrier that will someday be replaced by a cure.

That the disease played a part in my life made it especially difficult when I saw Woody finally begin to experience its symptoms. He had always been the steady rock I leaned upon. And when I began to see helplessness in his eyes, the look of a man lowering into the pit of its unique anguish, it broke my heart. He had for more than a year managed to avoid its stinging grasp. But how do you stay dry when you've been thrown into the ocean? Clinicians have shown that the symptoms of depression can be created in *healthy* lab rats by subjecting them to lengthy and hopeless scenarios. Woody had indeed—especially as our (pipe) dream of a stem cell rescue began to fade—been subjected to a long and hopeless scenario.

It happened not long after he'd given up on the De-Walt battery clip. When he knew his tools would no longer serve him, he had no way to preoccupy himself. A photographer friend of mine, Janet Litton, had come over one Saturday afternoon to take some pictures of Joe and Woody in the backyard. I'd noticed though that Woody's smile didn't come as easily. It would show up when he was with Joe and me, in our proximity, but when I saw him by himself, the smile faded, the energy drifted. His eyes would come to rest on things that didn't matter, as though he was seeing something else.

When Janet took a break and went into the house, and Joe wandered off somewhere, I asked him if he was feeling okay. We were sitting in the hanging lounge chair he'd bought for the new deck. He thought for a long moment, then looked at me apologetically and typed, "DEPRESSED."

I knew it was coming, but seeing him put the word on his LightWRITER hit me hard. I took his hand, wrapped it in mine. I had seen depression in other people, plenty of other people, friends, friends of friends—but seeing my dad experience it was devastating. It was the one thing I most wanted to protect him from, since I'd been powerless to stop any of the other demons that came ripping through his life. In hindsight, it was stupid to have thought I could shield him, given what he was facing, given the places I'm sure his mind went in the dark and quiet hours of the night.

We went to see the doctor later that day, and Woody started taking an antidepressant along with the surfeit of medications he was already consuming. And I think it lightened some of the pain. But with depression—as has been my experience—reality must provide *something* to grasp, something positive, anything, some news, large or small, significant or not, *something* that can lift the mind, if even just a little to allow the brain's chemistry to stabilize. In Woody's case, any infrequent benign news was always followed by another crushing blow, another new limit to his life, something else taken away.

The following weekend, we had haircuts scheduled, Woody and I. Henry and Joe weren't going with us this time, so I figured it was a good time to talk about some of the more difficult things, the specifics about his impending death.

The 405 South was uncharacteristically wide open on the way to Brentwood, so I had less time to steel myself to broach the subject. We talked about Henry and Joe, the usual stuff. And then we were in Brentwood. During which, I'd lost my nerve. I couldn't start a conversation about his death.

After we'd taken turns in Tom's barber chair, we got in the car and headed back to Studio City.

"I put the gun away," I said, venturing into the deeper end. "In a strong box, in the safe."

"GOOD."

"You didn't use it because you didn't have enough strength anymore?" I asked. "In your fingers?" I glanced over at him and caught his eye. He thought about it a moment, and then acknowledged that wasn't the real reason. He typed, "DIDN'T WANT HENRY AND JOE TO FIND OUT."

I nodded.

I realized then the choice he'd made. He abandoned the quicker (some would say more sensible) way out, so that his grandsons wouldn't have to learn how he'd died. The alternative he chose—the only option he knew of at the time—was what we had been told at UCLA; that the muscles around his lungs would eventually lose strength and slowly stop functioning. He would die by slow, gradual asphyxiation.

It was overwhelming to me, the decision he'd made. That he'd based it on the wellbeing of his two young grandsons (not the nightmare facing him) astounded me. While I don't know if at the time I realized the significance of that choice, I've since come to see it as heroic.

He had, by the way, earlier rejected another option suggested at UCLA—a breathing tube that was to be inserted by tracheotomy, so that a ventilator would permanently breathe for him, thereby prolonging his life. In Woody's eyes, however, it was more of a curse than a blessing, as it would have confined him *indefinitely* to a body that would soon become inert.

"I've been talking with one of the nurses at Hospice," I said, as we pulled onto Cantura Street, "and she promised me there's an easier way," meaning easier than slowly suffocating to death. I turned right, pulled into his driveway and stopped the car. "She said they'll make sure you have morphine. Enough so you can just go to sleep. You'll never know it."

He nodded. Then he picked up his LightWRITER

and typed, "THANK YOU."

Thank you, I thought. It seemed odd.

I reached over and took his hand again. And as the car engine cooled and the body's frame *ticked, ticked...* we sat there, holding hands. Behind us, Gordy walked by with his dog. Two houses over I could hear Timmy and Connor playing in the yard. I squeezed his hand and said, "I'll be with you through all of it." We were both close to tears while we listened to the world around us playing out, business as usual, like an unattended TV blathering in another room.

"I'm glad you didn't use the gun," I said.

He nodded slightly.

It was selfish on my part. Since his diagnosis, I'd been marking time, first in months, then weeks, then days. And there were still more days to be had, to be shared. Not many, but there were more, and I wanted them, those days, those hours, however many were left.

After a moment, I took a deep breath and opened the car door to get out. Then I had another thought, turned to him and smiled a little. "We should have a secret word. You and me."

He looked at me.

"You know, something you can use so I know it's you. Like if you try to contact me. Through Kenny. Later."

He thought about it, then took up his LightWRITER and typed a number. Four digits. "3847."

I studied the number a moment and then recognized the sequence. "Your PIN number?"

He smiled.

I laughed and we got out of the car.

FIFTEEN
Thursday

"Night falls; he has been swimming for hours, his strength almost gone; the ship, a distant far-off thing, where there were men, is gone; he is alone in the terrible gloom of the abyss; he sinks, he strains, he struggles, feels beneath himself invisible shadowy monsters; he screams." They are the words of Victor Hugo's unnamed man in *Les Miserables*, having fallen unseen off a ship that has since crested the ocean's curve. He is left to tread water in the dark, awaiting only his inevitable death.

On the Thursday morning of the week he died, there was something in his eyes, something different, not on the surface, but beneath the infrequent obligatory smile and the occasional half-hearted up-turned thumb. An acknowledgement perhaps of death's proximity. A resignation. But further still, in the depths of those tired eyes, there was fear. Something else I'd never seen in him. And it showed itself with each labored breath he took.

Neither was Oleta her usual chatty self when I stopped by that morning on my way to work. She walked me to the front door, as I was about to leave, and then took my arm to speak quietly. "He can't breathe when he lies down," she said. "Even with the bi-pap machine." She glanced back toward the TV room as dampness filled the bottom of her eyes. "He was up all night. Sitting in his desk chair. Trying to breathe. Trying to catch his breath. Just sitting there. All night."

"You're kidding," I said, at first irritated. "Why didn't you call me?"

She shook her head. "I didn't know. I didn't know until I got up."

I looked at her, letting it register.

"He didn't want to wake me," she added. "He didn't want to bother anyone."

So, while she slept, while I slept, while the world slept, he sat by himself through the empty hours of the night, struggling to breathe, gasping for air at times, knowing that the muscles around his lungs were finally failing. He was treading water on the open sea, his chin at its surface, his arms and legs giving out to exhaustion, death's shadow clasping his ankle, pulling him down.

"Goddamnit!" I said. "Goddamnit."

I called Hospice and they were at the house within the hour to set him up with morphine. They also arranged for an oxygen tank to be dropped off and set up, to help him breathe. Then I called the office and let them know what was happening, that I wasn't going to make it in to work.

He hadn't the strength to do much more than sit in his chair. With the morphine, hopefully, he'd be able to lie down and sleep. So I asked him if he wanted me to move his bed into the TV room. Oleta's room was just to the side of it, and I could sleep on the couch next to him. He considered the idea for a moment and nodded.

His bed though was a hospital rental, metal; not something I could drag through the house by myself. As it turned out, *Malcolm In The Middle* was shooting again a couple doors down, so I walked over and approached a few of the crew, who were hanging out near a truck, taking a break. When I pointed to my dad's house and told them I could use some help moving a heavy bed, the one smoking a cigarette took a last drag and dropped it on the pavement to grind out. "No problem," he said, as they headed toward Woody's house. What surprised me was they knew who Woody was and what was going on. I suppose it might've been idle chatter around the set. With the four of us, it took only a few minutes to get the bed dismantled, and then reassembled in the TV room.

Once the Hospice nurse showed up and the morphine was in my dad's system, with a steady flow of oxygen, Woody was indeed able to lie down and sleep soundly for what I thought would be his last night.

And sleep soundly he did, but it would not be his last night, nor his last surprise. The next morning, he woke refreshed, and told me to turn off the morphine. "DON'T NEED IT," he typed. He was breathing more easily with the oxygen and there was nearly a sparkle in his eye as he got out of bed, put on his robe and ambled over to his desk chair. I was slightly dumbfounded as I watched him turn on the computer and bring up a game of solitaire. He looked as perky as I'd seen him in weeks.

And, for the next two days, he rallied. He was there. He was alive.

They were two extraordinary days.

SIXTEEN

Friday and Saturday

There are a few times in life, and in death it turns out, when pieces of the universe drop into place, when the ball bounces the right way, when traffic lights turn green and cars flow unabated. The Friday and Saturday before he died were two such days. It is an odd thing to say, I know, about the vigil held for a loved one but, to me, those two days were an unexpected gift. They were extra hours to make sure the things that needed to be said were said, to see him with his friends, my friends, to cry together, to feel the warmth of his hand. All of it. And—given the relatively lousy cards he'd been dealt—I was amazed at how those two days seemed to blend bittersweet and laughter into a nectar that flowed around him like a warm blanket.

It was more like a slow-rolling social event than a deathwatch. The house was frequently bustling while, at other times, it was an ambling river, spinning out here and there in a kaleidoscope of every emotion. It was a patchwork quilt, miraculously sewn by happenstance. At the time, the events did not constitute a cohesive singular story, but rather a string of conjoining stories, each with its own build and zenith. And yet, there was a curious liquidity to the procession of visitors that, with the benefit of hindsight, presented a larger story. It was as if the comings and goings of friends and family had been orchestrated by some unseen conductor.

And maybe they were.

When Woody wasn't napping, there was always someone back in the TV room chatting with him, laughing with him, playing cards with him. At the same time, there were usually three or four of us hanging out in the living room, looking at pictures, telling jokes, playing with the slot cars.

There were so many who stayed, who dropped by, who drifted through, during those two remarkable days.

Harriett, the Hospice nurse, was a Godsend certainly. She was a vivacious, attractive and lusty woman in her forties who had, on several occasions, shared ribald jokes with Woody. He enjoyed seeing her arrive and, once or twice, if I'm not mistaken, appeared to be flirting with her.

Harriett loved it.

Hospice and the services they provide—I came to realize over the course of Woody's illness—are not about death. Rather, they are about the expansion of life, the embrace of what is left to live, no matter.

And Harriett was the embodiment of that philosophy.

Dr. Lee Kagan had been my physician and friend for maybe twenty or so years. He was also, coincidentally, the medical advisor for *Becker*. *And* he'd become my dad's doctor. In his early 50s, with salt and pepper hair, Lee had a smile that exuded an educated amusement with life. His own father—a holocaust survivor who came to America after the war—died of ALS just a few years earlier. So Lee was familiar with more than just the clinical aspects of the disease.

When my dad suffered from a bleeding ulcer some six months earlier, Lee showed up at the E.R. to make sure Woody was admitted and treated straightaway. And when it became difficult for us to get to his office, Lee started coming over to the house. So on that Friday, he made one last visit. One last house call.

When he walked into the TV room, he sat down opposite Woody, put his hands on Woody's knees and looked intently into his eyes. He spoke with a necessary directness, yet his tone was soft, gentle, imbued with kindness. Woody told him he had stopped taking his regiment of meds a couple of days earlier, and he had stopped taking in liquids and "eating" (through the G-tube). He was ready. Lee nodded and leaned over to unbutton Woody's shirt. Tenderly, he peeled the blood-pressure patch from Woody's chest and wadded it in his hand. He re-buttoned the shirt and they talked a few more moments. Finally, Lee smiled warmly, reached over to rest his hand on Woody's arm. Then he stood, hugged my dad and left.

There was Oleta, of course. She had been living there for the previous three months.

And Jodi. She was there in no small way. After all she, in the months leading up, had become quite close to Oleta and Woody, spending many afternoons at the house with them, helping Oleta and providing Woody with a troubled car to tinker with. Mary Randazzo too. She was Jodi's and my friend from the days when we all worked at MTM. When Jodi told Mary that Woody's condition had worsened, the two friends practically camped out at the house, leaving each evening late, to return the next morning.

Cath and the boys were in and out, along with Claudia, the boys' nanny. Part of the perennial tapestry of Woody's house. Some friends from work dropped by, since everyone knew what was going on.

On Friday, a beautiful leggy blond with an outspoken view on just about everything, came striding into the TV room and plopped herself down in front of Woody. Georgia McCreery was my assistant at a couple of different shows before becoming a writer in her own right. She was also a dear friend, and of course had become friends with Woody. As they talked, she thumbed through a photo album that was out and on his desk. When she came upon some pictures of him in his younger years, she gushed about how good-looking he was. She, by the way, has a voice that can command a room like an air raid siren. "Goddamn, Woody," she blared, "you were a fox! Hell, I woulda been all over that! All over that!"

I looked over and saw my dad soaking it up, beaming.

Gary Dontzig had certainly been through this ritual enough with the deaths of so many of his friends in the eighties. He came over to the house several times that weekend.

Another writer and friend from *Murphy Brown,* Norm Gunzenhauser, had gotten to know Woody, and dropped by to chat, to see if Woody had had a chance yet to watch the DVD Norm had given him on his birthday, back in

July—*The Vagina Monologues.* He hadn't. Norm was another guy who cracked Woody up. During the previous Christmas party at our house, Norm was sitting on the couch talking with my dad, while I was standing nearby. A gay friend of mine was about to leave and approached me to embrace and kiss me good-bye. Norm jabbed Woody's leg and yelled, "Hey, Woody! Look at that! Your son's gay!" Woody cracked up.

Other friends from the MTM days came by; Bruce Rasmussen and his wife Leslie. Both notoriously reticent in any given social situation. At the previous Christmas party, they sat together on another couch, just chatting with each other, no one else. Even still, they came by the house and sat with Woody, to talk for quite some time. At one point, Leslie looked over and noticed the black and white photo that came up on Woody's screensaver. "Is that you, Woody?" It was a shot of a young man with a wild head of dark hair, standing beside a beautiful fresh-faced young woman.

Woody nodded and typed out, "BERNICE." He was in love with her and had intended to marry her. When the war came, he enlisted in the Marines, with a promise to return. It never happened. He never saw her again.

I felt a need, at this juncture, to jump in with a little backstory for Bruce and Leslie about how Woody had Bernice's name tattooed on his left forearm. But, since I was little, he only ever had the one tattoo on his left forearm, and it did not say "Bernice." It was, as I mentioned earlier, the American Eagle on top of the Marine Corps' globe and anchor over the sweeping letters, "U.S.M.C." He'd always told me that he'd gotten the tattoo on shore leave after a few too many drinks and a challenge by his Marine Corps buddies. The truth, I'd only just learned after my mother's death, was that this iconic tribute to the Corps was a very conscious, *and wise*, decision to cover the smaller tattoo that proclaimed his love for Bernice.

My best friend from college, Craig, flew out from Las Vegas. Woody had become something of a surrogate grandfather to Craig and Katie's four kids; Carly, Mary, Francie and Andy. Since they never knew their own grandfathers, Woody seemed to fill that gap. And he loved them. When he lived in Pahrump, he and my mother made many trips into Las Vegas to visit the Mc-Call brood. On one occasion, Woody showed up in his pickup with a massive two-story doll house that he'd built for the girls.

My dad always had a special place in his heart for Craig, not just because he was my best friend, but because he and Craig shared similar political views. I imagine Woody felt, during his time in Studio City, that Craig's occasional visits were islands of salvation amidst the vast sea of liberals he'd found himself surrounded by.

The boys were out in the back most often, or over at the neighbor's house playing, so their nanny Claudia spent her time indoors with Woody. She too had more or less adopted him, since she barely knew her own dad, and her family was not close. She was heartbroken over Woody's imminent death and like many of us, she was determined to squeeze in as much time as possible with him.

For his part, he was forever amused by her unabashed and brazen approach to just about everything.

She saw no barrier to, had no qualms with, explaining to Woody or Oleta or both—they were 78 and 76, respectively—exactly what was going on in her life, including her sex life. I suppose it was the sheer ingenuousness of her detailed accounts that was so disarming. Months earlier, I'd stopped by after work and found Oleta and Woody, each near tears from laughter because Claudia was assuring them, in her most sincere broken English, that she was not pregnant. *Not* pregnant! Even though her boyfriend, who usually took his dick out and came on her stomach, didn't take anything out during their last encounter, opting instead to come inside of her. *This* she explained without reservation to a couple of septuagenarians (if she'd had a smart phone, I'm sure she would have included a series of dick pix). Claudia took Woody and Oleta's laughter to mean they doubted the assessment she was giving them of her un-impregnated uterus, so she argued her point all the more. By the end of her staunch proclamation, Woody bet her $100 that she *was* pregnant.

As it turned out, a few weeks later, he lost the bet. And she collected.

On Saturday, she sat down with him and challenged him to a game of poker. Something they'd done fairly frequently over the last year or so. And as they played, her laughter filled the house, while he in turn was giggling and laughing at her, with her. Though I wasn't privy to much of their conversation, I suspect that what Woody found so funny was Claudia's ever-changing rules for the game.

Nearly ten years later, she wrote me an email to ask about the boys. Woody was still on her mind, as she wrote (in her inimitable style): "That old man really was special and will be always in my heart. I wish I could have (had) more time to enjoy him. For me, he is the only father I ever had. I still talk about him. He was so sweet. That old man really got to me. I miss him. Claudia."

Woody's younger brother, Charlie, looks a lot like Woody.

He and his wife Barbara—a mousy-looking woman with an authoritative tone that grates like metal on metal—were on their way to LAX from the Bay Area, headed for a vacation in China. They came by the house for a couple of hours to see Oleta and Woody.

To say good-bye.

A third brother, the eldest, Leon, was shot and killed in 1965. An investigator for Southern Pacific Railroad, he was looking into a complaint about kids throwing rocks at trains in the San Francisco Bay Area. As he approached one of the suspects' houses, a 16-year-old boy opened the front door holding a shotgun, and pumped a round into Leon's stomach. I was ten at the time and not allowed to visit him in the ICU, where he fought to stay alive for over a week. I remember only the vigil held at my grandmother's house in Oakland.

Charlie had hand written a series of stories about their youth together, the four siblings. As he held the yellow-lined paper at arm's length and read one story after the next, my dad and his sister laughed at events they had long forgotten, jumping in with additions to the stories—memories of a mule that wouldn't respond to any command; mean tricks their older brother Leon played on the only girl, Oleta; a rope swing over a nearby creek that eventually broke; mischief that mistakenly brought punishment to the wrong person; a first car that had no keys. As Charlie read the stories, Woody seemed to lose himself in their immediacy, his mind no longer in Studio City. For those moments he was back in the small Texas town where they all grew up. He was laughing with his siblings, twice to the point of tears.

Charlie and Barbara's visit, however, was not all sweet memories.

There was a moment, a comment, presented by wife Barbara that I heard about—after the fact, after she and Charlie were off to LAX and then China—that astounded me for its lack of sensitivity, for its incredible...what, stupidity?

Barbara, whom I didn't know from my adult years, sat down near my dad to talk with Catherine about their vacation plans. Fully within Woody's earshot, she said to Cath, "If he passes in the next couple of days, don't call us over there. Wait until we get home. We don't want our vacation interrupted."

As I learned later, Barbara was someone my dad was never fond of, the same way others in the family were not fond of my mother. (Which made me realize that the brothers perhaps had more in common than I suspected.)

Joe and Henry both had soccer games that Saturday. It was one of the few that Woody missed. The games were usually held at a small park called Beeman, maybe a mile from his house.

Since he couldn't make it to either of the games, I

decided to take the camera over to the park and get a few shots of the boys playing. When I got back to the house, I announced that I got some great stuff. After I downloaded the pictures onto his computer, he scrolled through them, pleased, then reached for his LightWRITER and typed, "WHO WON?"

"Oh," I said, "I don't know." He looked at me curiously. It was a look I recognized from my youth when he'd send me off to the garage to retrieve, say, a half-inch box wrench. I'd go and look. And look and look. Until finally he'd come to find me, where I'd be *still* staring at the pegboard with its myriad hanging tools, and he'd say, "Russell T.! What in the hell ya doin'?"

"Looking for the half-inch box wrench."

And he'd say, "You mean this?" Then he'd reach to the wall in front of me and lift the half-inch box wrench.

That was the look.

He wasn't able to use her services the week before, and he missed her. More to the point, he missed her touch. Kimberly had been Woody's masseuse for over a year. She was maybe 30, scrappy, a survivor, having had to battle for every break she'd ever gotten in life. Awkward, even a little peculiar in conversation, she had a hard personality, but an emanating soft spot for Woody. She took great pride in her ability to adjust to his ever capricious and fragile condition. Aside from that, she'd grown to care deeply about him, to love him. A week earlier, she'd come by for their usual appointment, but Woody was starting to have trouble breathing when he lay down. On Saturday she stayed for a while to visit with him and Oleta, but there was no massage that day. There would be no more massages.

Kimberly had become a weekly luxury for him the summer he moved to Los Angeles. The "massage" was a phenomenon unknown to him prior to his move, but one that he embraced wholeheartedly once he discovered it. We had gone up to Ventura for the weekend, where we had a house on the beach. Some other friends were with us and, for some reason, the subject of massages came up. Woody mentioned that he'd never had one.

We Angelinos were shocked. Mortified, I tell you.

I called a local masseuse who came out to the house and set up her table in a guest room downstairs. When she was ready, Woody followed me downstairs, where he was told to strip down to his underwear and get comfortable. He looked tentatively at me, uncertain about this whole frou-frou endeavor and then prepared himself for his first massage.

An hour and change later, he emerged from the stairway into the living room, looking a little unsteady. He wobbled over to rejoin us at the table. He had a smile on his face that looked a little like Elmer Fudd's after Bugs might've whacked him in the head with a frying pan. A moment later, he reached for some paper and a pen to write (this was before the LightWRITER), "If I'd known about that when I was younger, I wouldn't have wasted my money on booze and cigarettes."

On his last Saturday, Kimberly stayed for a couple of hours, reluctant to say good-bye, until finally she had to. She kissed him gently, said she loved him and then walked slowly out to her car. As she opened her car door, she turned and looked back at Woody's house, tears streaking her cheeks.

Given the influx and flow of friends and family, it was a rare moment when the two of us, Woody and I, were alone together. During one such moment, however, I asked if he still wanted to be buried at the military cemetery in Nevada, next to my mother. I'm not sure why I asked since everything had already been arranged. I guess I had the sneaking suspicion that he might want something different. Maybe because my mother had been so seldom mentioned, or maybe it was the picture of Bernice on his computer desktop. I don't know. But I asked.

He thought about it. Then he typed, "TEXAS."

"Texas? You mean...Texas?"

He nodded and typed, "MOM & DAD." His parents had been buried in Boonesville, Texas. He wanted his ashes to be buried at the foot of their graves.

I nodded and assured him it would happen, knowing in the back of my mind that it might cause a problem with the cemetery in Nevada. After all, it was a military cemetery and my mother (never in the military) had already taken up residence.

I was becoming oddly used to these pragmatic talks with him about his death. That he did not shy away from them made things easier for me. In the same way, his decision to stop driving came as soon as he began to have trouble holding his head up. He simply handed me his car keys and typed that he shouldn't drive anymore. The following week, when Oleta returned from Arizona, he sold her his car for $1.

The issue of his driving had been looming in the back of my mind. I knew the time was coming when he'd no longer be able to safely drive, and I was steeling myself for a difficult conversation. Not that he would have fought me on it—just that I hated the idea of hurting his feelings, of infantilizing him. I realize many with aging parents are not so fortunate. When one parent or the other clings tenaciously to what they see as their last means of independence, the remaining time together is often laced with resentment. For some, it means the dissolution of equanimity at a time when equanimity is vital to the fragile process of saying goodbye.

In the last few nights of his life, Woody and I were up many times to make the trip to the bathroom. He'd not had any liquids, but as Dr. Kagan explained, his body was ridding itself of everything; preparing itself for death. He was miserable and weak and could barely stand by himself. So, after I walked him to the bathroom, and helped him undo his pants in front of the toilet, I'd hold his arm and wait for him to urinate. The process was humiliating for him, but less so than when his sister had to perform the task.

The mind goes to many peculiar places in the midst of a situation like this. As I stood holding his frail arm, listening to him pee, it occurred to me that I had not seen his penis in, what, forty-plus years? Since I was little and I used to climb into the tub with him. And I remember thinking then that it was enormous. E-normous. And throughout the years, the decades—well after I came to understand the perceived significance of such things—it remained enormous in my mind.

Except...

As I stood there beside him and caught sight of it again, I thought...well, it's an average penis. Nothing to be ashamed of, but certainly nothing in the realm of the anaconda I'd mentally manufactured. And so vanished the myth where, in its absence, a son was pleased and somewhat grateful to learn that his own penis was in the same relative size-range as his father's.

It was then that I remembered an incident a few months earlier when a twenty-something babysitter named Britney showed up at the house to watch the boys. Upon meeting her, Joe stepped up to Britney and, for some unknown reason, announced, "My dad's penis is gigantic!" Awkward, yes—and difficult to smoothly shift to a conversation about emergency phone numbers—but God bless the little guy.

During one of the more quiet moments on Saturday, I passed through the TV room where Woody was asleep on his bed, a dull brown blanket draped over him. I stood and looked at him for a long moment. Then quietly, gently, I climbed up onto the bed and moved in behind him, to spoon. I slid my left arm softly over his shoulder, careful not to put pressure on his breathing. To my surprise, he was not asleep. He shifted slightly and reached up to gently rub my arm. Then he slid his hand down over my watch to my hand and held it.

And there we lay.

It was one of many small consolations to weigh against the baleful twilight, a tiny gift to be realized and taken into the heart, to be cherished above its smallness. To those who lose a loved one suddenly, unexpectedly, there are not these conscious gifts. When there's no good-bye, no warning, when the loss is sudden and un-expected, the pain must be all the more lonely. There is then only the possible memory of having appreciated each other when the finish line was a mere fictional player in the distance. During these months with my dad, I was beginning to realize that it isn't often done. We don't take the time to recognize those around us while they're still around us. I suppose it is the one re-sounding lesson I came away with. It is, admittedly, not a huge revelation, not greatly profound—nonetheless, it is the lesson that became, for me, the most significant.

And as I lay there with my dad, Oleta crossed through the room and stopped when she saw us. She studied us a moment and sighed. "Well, bless your hearts," she said.

Later on Saturday—as Woody was losing energy, looking worn—his young friend Trent arrived. Striding into the TV room with his usual brazen gusto, he belted out, "Woody!" My dad turned and brightened. Trent, his arms wide, bent to Woody and gingerly embraced him. Then he sat to visit. Woody had a couple of things he'd been meaning to show Trent on the computer—dirty jokes from his friends Elmer and Noel.

Later; after Jodi, Mary and I wandered into the TV room with Oleta, I saw that Trent was gone. But as I started to cross through the darkened living room, I realized he wasn't. He was sitting quietly by the front window, crying.

As a comedy writer, I've often contended that a serious situation needs only the addition of something small, something relatively insignificant, to make it funny. Pope Benedict XV, lying in state, with a Slinky in his hand. Winston Churchill addressing the valiant Londoners of the coming blitzkrieg...but his zipper is down. Like that.

Thanks to the morphine drip, throughout Friday and Saturday, Woody was able to take naps whenever he wanted. And after he had rested, he'd move from his bed to his desk chair, while I moved the oxygen tank and its clear plastic tube with him. At one point, he indicated that I run the tubing in a circuitous route from the tank to him because, apparently, a couple of visitors, when they sat down to talk with him, had rested a foot on the tubing.

The tube however, though pushed well out of the way, inevitably moved with his movement, and eventually another visitor innocently rested his foot on it. This time, though, Woody was prepared; he pushed a button on the LightWRITER to bring up a message he'd already entered. The machine's synthetic voice blurted, "GET YOUR FOOT OFF THE FUCKING HOSE."

On an occasion when we were quietly sitting together, Woody reached over and rested his hand on mine. I smiled and studied it, the skin that stretched like thin crinkled paper over his long bones, frail now, ephemeral. Then I looked up and saw that he was looking at me, studying me as well, the way one studies a cherished memento or a coin before it's tossed from the side of a ship. The way one looks at someone they'll never see again.

I said, "I love you, my dad."

He smiled back, looking at the corners of my eyes, my ear, my chin, soaking in what he could. Absorbing.

Then he released my hand and turned to lift the LightWRITER from his desk. He set it on his lap and typed, hunt-and-peck as usual. I looked down at it as he pushed the button to make it speak.

It said, "I LOVE YOU MY SON ALWAYS AND ALWAYS WILL."

SEVENTEEN
Sunday

The cupcake wrappers were lying in the cool grass of his front lawn. Light yellow, dull blue, dreary green. I studied the first, lining up Woody's driver behind it. Bill Murray's voice played in my head, this time from *Caddyshack:* "Cinderella story...outta nowhere...former greens keeper about to become the Masters champion..." *Thwack!* A few blades of grass flew into the air, as the dented cupcake wrapper popped up, twirled and floated back to the lawn.

It was Sunday. There was nothing left to do.

Woody woke that morning to a body without power, miserable, barely able to move. He, we, had been many times to the bathroom that night, each time taking more effort. By the time a Hospice nurse came by in the morning, he was ready to leave. I told the nurse to turn up the morphine, let him sleep...until he was gone.

Now there was nothing to do but wait, to stand on the platform and peer down the empty rails at a shrinking train. I'd hoped it would come sooner rather than later. In one respect, I was relieved that I would no longer have to share looks with someone who knew he was drowning. I would miss him, but I wouldn't miss seeing the anguish in his eyes.

Mary and Jodi were there, Gary had come back. I

grabbed a box of cupcake wrappers from the kitchen, took one of Woody's drivers from his golf bag in the garage and walked out to the front yard to practice my swing.

We learned to play golf together, my dad and I, many years earlier. In Salinas. I was fourteen and angry that we lived in Salinas—a town we had only just moved to, a place I considered cold, emotionally void. But once every couple of weeks, my dad would take me out to the links, and we'd play nine or eighteen holes.

By fifteen, I'd forgotten about golf. We were then living in Fair Oaks, near Sacramento, and my interests had moved on to things that didn't include my father. He stayed with golf and grew to love it (though it was not all that often he could get out with his buddies to play, since it meant leaving my mother at home). When he did play, he and Elmer and Noel made the most of it, often spending as much time at the *nineteenth* hole as at the others combined.

When Woody first moved to Studio City, I was pleased that his house was only a few blocks from Studio City Golf and Tennis. It was a nine-hole "pitch 'n' putt," practically walking distance, that he could have popped over to anytime. Unfortunately, he never did. After the move, he put his clubs in the garage and never took them out. The ALS, he said, had taken away his "rhythm." So on the last Friday of his life, I promised him I would take up the game again. I'd learn it, I said, and I'd do so with his clubs. He nodded and seemed pleased with that.

Thwack! I swung at another cupcake wrapper. He'd been asleep most of the day. How long now would we spend in this no man's land? Waiting for the train to disappear? How long before he'd finally stop breathing?

By six o'clock it was over.

I had come back into the living room where Jodi and Mary were sitting with Gary. Catherine was in the kitchen, the boys in Oleta's room watching a video. Oleta stepped into the living room and told us he was gone. She said he took a breath, smiled a little and then his face just relaxed.

I was relieved. And mildly heartened to learn of his smile.

That I wasn't in the room with him when he died hardly seemed significant to me. Though I suppose there is something special in that moment, something magical even, I was just glad to know it was over. I had spent so much time watching him slide toward the abyss that the final drop into it seemed unimportant to me.

What I did experience, in the moment I learned that he was dead, was a feeling that something was strangely familiar. It seemed peculiar to me how frequently life's largest transitions happened on schedule—death and birth, adolescence, old age—regardless of our effort or intent. In that way, Woody's death felt wildly similar to the births of Henry and Joe. I remember thinking how odd it was that we have no prior experience, no working knowledge of how these monumental and complex transitions are accomplished. Yet we nonetheless find ourselves intimately engaged in them, like cogs on a wheel within an immense machine, mere passengers, witnesses to a functioning system as old as time. While tiny Henry was positioning his body for birth, Catherine's body was preparing to expel it. Likewise, Woody's body had readied itself for death, shutting down systems and discarding fluids the way a doomed aircraft jettisons fuel before impact. And when everything had been readied, the prerequisites met, life and death just seemed to happen.

Catherine came in from the kitchen, as we all stepped into the TV room. Woody's head had fallen to the side, his dentures were loose, like they were about to fall out. I rolled a towel and put it around his neck to hold his head and chin up. A little dignity.

His face was still drawn, elongated. There was peacefulness. Oleta stepped up beside me, put an arm around my waist and looked at him with me. "You know," she said, as we studied his face, "I never saw it before, but he looks so much like Grandpa Holley." It was true. I'd seen pictures of my great grandfather, Wesley Holley (Arabelle's father), and suddenly the resemblance was uncanny. It had emerged, I suppose, with the relaxation of the muscles in Woody's face.

It was an odd coincidence (perhaps), but a few days later, after I'd checked on Henry and Joe and was about to turn the lights out in their room, I was struck by what I saw in Joe's somnolent, relaxed face. It was the face of *his* grandfather. It was unmistakable.

I'd never seen it before. Or since.

I sat down next to Woody's body and put my hand on his arm as the heat slowly drifted from it. I rested my ear against the watch on his wrist, the watch he was so proud of because it lit up, a Timex, and because it cost so much less than the watch I was wearing. A fact he delighted in and pointed out whenever I had to send mine in for repairs.

As I sat there with his lifeless body, I found myself thinking about when I was small and he would arrive home from work. I would rush to him, sit on top of his foot and wrap my arms around his leg, so that he could drag me through the living room. I thought about when we would go to the drive-in movies, and he would announce, "All we need now is that sack of rotten potatoes!" And then he'd toss a blanket over my head, pick me up and throw me over his shoulder to carry me out to the car like a sack of rotten potatoes.

I reached up and put my hand on his forehead near his hairline, like the way you do when someone's sick. There was still warmth, but it was growing cooler. The heat, the energy of his life force, was floating out from its home, wafting away with his soul toward forever. That thing that was him was no longer.

In that moment, I felt no particular attachment to his body, to what remained. It seemed useless. It had become a shell that I nearly resented, and only wanted to see gone. It had betrayed my father, taunted him, tortured him, and now it was merely taking up space, taunting *me*.

Henry and Joe were still watching a video in my aunt's bedroom. I opened the door and stepped in, closing it gently behind me. I told them that Grampa had died. They looked at me for a moment, but I don't think it sank in. Or maybe they were expecting it. They may have been so (over) prepped about Grampa's impending death that they took it in stride. In the months to come, though, they would revel in recalling stories about Grampa. "Remember when Grampa took us to the movies?" "Remember when we used to sleep over at Grampa's house?" "Remember when he made pancakes and bacon?"

When I talked to Catherine, we agreed it was best that she take the boys out the other door and home, so that they would not see the body. I don't think it would have been traumatic for them, but I didn't know what they would think. Maybe I was reacting to my own feelings—that I didn't want to see it, that I wanted "it" to be gone.

Around 8 p.m., a white van backed into the driveway. A middle-aged man got out and walked to the front door. We shook hands as he introduced himself, handing me paperwork on a clipboard that needed to be filled out. He sat down in the living room—with me and Oleta, Jodi, Mary and Gary—while I filled out the paperwork. Under the section about the burial, I wrote that the ashes were to be shipped back to me and then they'd be taken to Texas for burial with his parents.

This, I knew, would not sit well with the folks at the military cemetery in Nevada. And, sure enough, a couple weeks later I got a phone call from an unfortunate clerk in their offices: "Uh, Mr. Woody, we understand that your father requested to be buried in Texas. Is that right?"

"Yeah. Boonesville, Texas." I knew where the guy was going with this, but I didn't feel like helping him out. I acted like I had no idea what he was talking about.

"Well, uh, that presents something of a problem here...since this is a *military* cemetery, you see...and your mother is buried here, and she never actually, uh, served."

My fear, of course, was that the cemetery would want to send her back to me. So I continued to feign ignorance, bordering on out-and-out stupidity and, by the end of the conversation, I pretended to be just as stumped for a solution as the poor guy on the phone. It was perhaps immature on my part, definitely petty—I mean, certainly I understood the dilemma—but I felt like, at that stage of the game, at that stage of my life, I had dealt with my mother enough, now she was someone else's problem.

I knew his body would have to be moved. Carried out to the van, one man at each end of it. And when the driver turned to me and asked if I'd help him do so, I said I would, but I was dreading it from deep within. I couldn't stand the thought of lifting Woody's limp frame and hauling it out like an oversized rag doll. Mostly I dreaded the thought of seeing one of his lifeless arms drop from his side like a piece of spaghetti. I don't know what it was, but the thought of it was suddenly more than I could bear.

Gary saw it in my face. He stood up and said to the guy, "That's okay, I'll help."

I was grateful.

And as they moved into the other room to retrieve the body, Jodi and Mary offered to go for a walk with me, so I wouldn't have to see it happen. On the dark sidewalk of Cantura, we walked arm-in-arm, the three of us, past the ever vigilant poplars that lined the street, down to the end of the block. Then, as we turned around to head back, the white van slowly glided out of the driveway, turned and ambled past us. We stopped and watched as it did.

I waved. "Good-bye, Dad."

I didn't feel unfortunate or cheated by his illness and death. I felt more satisfied than anything else. That there had been no wasted time. That we took greedily—he from what remained of his life; the laughter of his grandchildren; the generosity of the *Becker* cast and crew, including its star; the touch of the people who loved him; and I took from him—every moment we had available to us. Had we not, had *I* not, I would have been grieving for a journey untraveled, for the small moments lost. It was, after all, an adventure of the heart, my heart; an adventure that may be rivaled one day, but never topped.

In that regard, I pitied my brother and his choice, his choices, his lack of energy or maybe his lack of wherewithal to endure. I don't know his deepest reason or reasons, but whatever it was, whatever they were, whatever stopped him from taking part in those 17 months, he missed one of life's most significant odysseys.

From my perspective, I had only a single grievance throughout the ordeal, though small and hardly worthy of sympathy: I wished I could have spent more time with him as *two adults*—me not being his child, he not being mine. Just two guys. For whatever reason, whatever logic, he spent those years with my mother, and I spent them *away* from my mother.

A handful of times, when I was in college and he was still working at PG&E, I would meet up with him and his buddies, Noel and Elmer, for lunch in Sacramento. They were long lunches, as I recall, more liquid than solid, more funny than serious. I loved being with him like that; when he was not being a father, when I was not being a son. Just a couple of guys laughing with Noel and Elmer.

That laughter with his buddies, I have to admit, was seldom mature laughter. There was an amusing dynamic that surfaced when he was around those two. One particular "phase" they went through just after I'd finished college involved any one of them standing casually next to another and leaning into them as though sharing a secret—then strategically tapping that sensitive area of the male anatomy just hard enough to cause the other pain. The perpetrator would then move away, as though unaware of any transgression, and watch the victim struggle to regain his dignity. I hadn't been around a level of behavior like that since, well, junior high school.

I know he paid dearly for those infrequent "lunches" by returning home a little later than usual, a little more unsteady than he should have been. But the ones I was able to share with him, I cherished.

The V-neck undershirts in his chest of drawers, they all smelled like him. Familiar. Safe.

I didn't feel like going home, didn't feel like going to sleep. So I wandered the house, poking through his stuff. There was energy, his energy, in everything. In his ratty green terry cloth bathrobe, its pockets still stuffed with Kleenex. In his closet, his shirts, his pants, his boots, the ones that were given to him by his older brother's widow, the brother that was killed in the '60s.

A couple of ties that hung lifelessly near the back of the closet; one paisley, one striped, left over from the days when his work required such things. All of it was him, its meaning different now that he was gone. Likewise, it fascinated me, the haphazard way he had tossed his loose change on the dresser; his bundle of keys, the way they came to rest beside his worn leather wallet at that certain angle—all of it a commonplace occurrence a week earlier, now forever beyond replication.

I stepped into the garage and pulled open, with a raw *clunk,* a drawer of his beaten rollaway tool chest, gunmetal blue, older than I. Before me was a splay of grease-smeared wrenches, screwdrivers, a claw hammer, some loose screws and ten-penny nails that rolled back and forth with the movement of the drawer. It was a collage assembled by random accumulation and necessity, a testament to his knowhow, his pluck, to his ability to improvise.

Oleta had long since gone to bed, so I was alone in the early morning hours as they crept in and enveloped me. In the TV room, a rumpled beige sheet lay at the foot of his abandoned bed, a corner of it draping to the floor like pale funeral bunting. I sat on the carpet, rifling through the files of his desk drawer and saw that he was more organized than I thought. There was a file folder for each utility, each neatly filled with bills paid in chronological order. And there, to my surprise, amongst the more mundane file labels was one that said "J.A.G." His favorite TV show.

Some months earlier, Catherine and I bought him a "walk-on" part at an auction for Henry and Joe's school. Woody was thrilled to learn that he was going to the set of *J.A.G.*

When I came by his house early on the morning of the shoot, he was feeling spry and looking forward to his day of work as a "Naval Hospital Patient." (The exteriors of the hospital were shot on a remote location at the other side of the San Fernando Valley.) When we got there, a director's chair was waiting for him with his name on it, along with a bag of gifts—*J.A.G.* swag, if you will—a *J.A.G.* hat and sweat shirt, autographed photos, a bumper sticker. He sat in the chair and assessed his booty with the glee of a kid at Christmas, while I walked over to give my phone number to one of the production assistants, before I left for work.

When I returned, an attractive woman was standing in front of him, talking about something, looking at something he'd typed on the LightWRITER. She turned and extended her hand to me, said her name was Catherine. I didn't know who she was, but she seemed nice. And beautiful. A moment later, one of the crew tapped her shoulder and said she was due in wardrobe. She said good-bye to both of us and moved off. When I turned back to my dad, he was looking at me like he'd raised an idiot.

"What?" I said.

He typed, "THAT'S THE STAR!" Meaning, "That's Catherine Bell, the star, *you moron!*" He was dumbfounded that I didn't know who she was.

Around three a.m., I plucked another of my dad's drivers from his golf bag (I don't know why—I just wanted something of his), and I wandered out of the house over to Ventura Boulevard. The street was empty, illuminated by the glow of L.A.'s reflective night sky and the buzzing amber streetlamps within the long line of towering palms. But as I passed a hodgepodge of darkened storefront windows and caught glimpses of myself on the sidewalk—holding a golf club—it occurred to me that my decision to take it with me was not the wisest of choices. I was, after all, a grubby looking un-shaven man in a slovenly un-tucked shirt, slinking past the massive glass fronts of boulevard shops in the wee hours of the morning—*holding a fucking golf club!* My mind jumped to the squealing of tires, the flaring of squad car doors with guns propped over them, and the squawk of a cop's bullhorn demanding that I put the weapon down and place my hands on my head.

No cops came by.

As I walked, I found myself talking to my dad. I said I was sorry he had to go through what he went through, sorry that I couldn't do anything to stop it, to protect him from the suffering. I thanked him for facing it so bravely, for remaining so loving, for treating those of us around him with such regard.

Near the intersection of Ventura and Laurel Canyon Boulevards, I stepped into the gutter and sat on the sidewalk. The streets were desolate, noiseless, a scene set by Stephen King. The traffic lights changed again and again, playing out to the night their pointless light show.

Finally I cried.

On only a handful of occasions had I ever cried without the accompanying pain of depression. This was one such occasion. It was different. It was clean. As though each sob was the expulsion of something weighty and unwanted. It was like clearing leaves from a rain gutter or sludge from a sink.

It felt good.

The following Monday afternoon, I stood on the floor of Stage 31, facing the diner set with Woody's LightWRITER and a wrinkled paper bag in my hand. Dave Hackel was standing next to me with his hand on my shoulder. After the run-through he'd gathered the cast and crew, the writers, everyone. They formed a large semi-circle in front of us.

"My dad died yesterday," I said, sure that they knew it anyway. "So...he typed a message on Saturday." I was determined not to break down in front of everyone. "He wanted me to play it for you." I pushed the speak button on the machine and the familiar mechanical monotone played out, "TED AND HATTIE AND SAVERIO AND ALL OF BECKER, THANK YOU FOR BEING SO NICE TO ME. IT WAS A GOOD YEAR. MY LOVE TO YOU ALL."

While some started to cry, I was holding steady. Steady, that is, until I too expressed my gratitude to everyone for their kindness over the past year. Then my voice cracked and broke, hot tears were suddenly streaming down my face, snot from my nose. My vain and futile hope of presenting myself as a manly man, a grown-up, disintegrated into soggy sniffling and a staccato of high-pitched words.

I tried as best I could to compose myself, to regain a little decorum, to show the steadiness my dad might have. I didn't succeed, though I did manage to eke out that it had not been *only* sadness and gloom over the few days leading up to his death, that there were lighter moments, even funny moments. And then I told them about—and played for them—Woody's directive to un-aware visitors: "GET YOUR FOOT OFF THE FUCKING HOSE!"

With a deep breath, I regained some volume to my voice and explained that, for the past few months, Woody's feet had been swollen, so he started wearing a pair of old tattered leather slippers. Everywhere. Including the last few filmings of the show that he was able to attend. When Ted saw him wearing the slippers, he told Woody that they were the "nicest slippers" he'd ever seen, and that he wanted to know where Woody got them, so he could get himself a pair. I took the slippers out of the paper bag and handed them to Ted. Woody'd penned a note on top of one: "Ted, you said you wanted these. Love, Woody."

The next day, I rented a car and drove north to visit a few of the houses I grew up in. To unwind. To think. To wallow.

Walnut Creek.

Red Bluff.

Oakland.

When I returned, there was a small memorial at Woody's house. Nothing extravagant. More like a get-together. Woody's young friend Trent had put together a video of Woody's old pictures, backed by music.

But there were no speeches.

I didn't feel the need.

Everything had been said. *To* him.

In the end—like each of us—he'd had more than many could hope for, less than many who can be pointed to.

But, all in all, he was happy in his life.

He found pleasure in the average day. He got joy from the fact that he was good at his job. He loved fixing things, working on cars, helping people out. He delighted in spending time with his friends and, dare I say it, he probably found satisfaction in the relative stability of his marriage.

But then, he didn't *expect* happiness. That is often, I suppose, why certain people are happy in their lives, despite what others might see as a paucity of things to be happy about. He always seemed to enjoy just being. He seemed never to want or expect more than he had.

Perhaps it's why *I,* in turn, never felt cheated by the limited time I had with him, because I never expected to have it in the first place. And, with the ticking clock of ALS, the time I *did* spend with him was all the more intense. It forced me to recognize everything, to say everything, and that was a blessing.

It also forced me to see my world and those I love as fleeting, to see them as pieces of history that one day will be viewed only from afar. It forced me to collect significant moments, to savor them, to store them in the folds of my mind.

The night *Becker* was given an award by the MDA at the Beverly Hilton was filled with those moments. To express my feelings for my dad, *about* my dad, across a sea of well-dressed strangers—while he was there to hear it—is a moment and memory most cherished.

EIGHTEEN
Heroes

Becker's cast and producers were all on the stage when Ted took the podium that night. He swiveled to either side, looking for me. "Russ? Come on over here." As I moved up and stood beside him, he turned back to the microphone and the audience. "This year for us was made incredibly special by Russ sharing his father, Woody, with us. Woody was diagnosed with ALS a year ago, and Russ and his wife, Catherine, brought him out to California to be with them. And they do...well..." he said as he turned to me. "You do father and son so well that you have inspired all of us. You make us laugh, you make us cry, you make us feel good about what we do." He shaded his eyes then and looked out into the audience. "Woody?" Then, "Yes, I see you raising your hand," he said. "You make me miss my daddy. It's a joy for all of us to be here to honor you. You've made our year really special, Woody."

As Ted stepped aside, I moved in front of the microphone and looked out into the same bright lights: "When we were first thinking about doing this episode, I asked my dad what he thought of a story about a patient of Dr. Becker's, a nice older guy who has ALS. Then Becker gets him a LightWRITER to help him speak... and he turns into an asshole. Woody laughed and gave me a thumbs up."

I explained that we used a bit of creative license in writing the part—that Woody wasn't really so bad. In fact, to me, I said, he was a hero. Both in small ways, and in big ways:

"During the Second World War, he was a Marine serving in the Pacific on a battleship called the *USS Nevada*. At the height of the war, at the height of Japan's desperation, a kamikaze pilot nose-dived and full-throttled for the bridge of my father's ship. My dad's battle station was in the gun turret just below the bridge, so he and his fellow Marine gunners swung their 20 mm guns at the oncoming plane and started firing for all they were worth. A couple of seconds before the plane was to blast into the bridge of the ship and into my father's battle station, its wing shattered from the artillery fire, the plane dipped to the left and blasted into the battle station just past the ship's bridge." The details of this story, I told the audience, I'd only just learned a few months earlier.

I said then that I had another example of my dad's heroism, and told the story of when I was 13 and struggling in futility to knot a necktie before my first dance. I explained how he stepped in and took me through the process. And now, whenever I stand in front of a mirror and tie a tie...I think of my dad. Then I said—because of the ALS—I had to help him put on *his* tie a few hours earlier.

I thanked the cast, the crew, of Becker, the other writers, yes for their talent and their effort, but mostly for the way they'd treated my father and me. And then I thanked Woody for his decision to be there, to be with us, his decision not to hide. I thanked him for his day-to-day courage in the face of the disease's relentless barrage of assaults.

And I thanked him for being my dad.

And for teaching me to tie a necktie.

Then I said, "I love you, Dad."

It was a moment in time that will always stay with me, but it was not the most significant of the evening. That moment was still to come, as so often the most important things aren't planned, include no pinned metal, no ribbon-cutting scissors. The most significant moments take place elsewhere, beyond the lights, where they can be easily overlooked. Like the beauty of a perfect leaf plucked from the porch, they require the effort to recognize them.

As the ceremony was breaking up and I made my way back to our table, guests were picking up coats, purses, etc., and ambling toward the exits. Except for the crowd that had gathered next to, and around, Woody. Perhaps fifteen or twenty people were waiting to meet him, to shake his hand, to hug him, to offer their kind thoughts.

On this night, he was a celebrity. The type people just wanted to touch.

As I wedged in around the side, a little closer to my dad, a slender woman in a black dress had put a hand on his shoulder and was thanking him for being there, for having the courage to do so.

As she moved away, I thought it was my chance to edge in next to him. But I was stopped when a barrel-chested man in his forties stepped between us, in front of me, facing Woody. He looked perhaps as uncomfortable in formal clothes as did my father. He was a large beefy man, with fists that swallowed Woody's hand as he took it in his. He was a firefighter from New York who had, a few months earlier, rushed into one of the World Trade Center buildings during the 9/11 attacks. He saved many lives before the building collapsed.

He took hold of Woody's shoulders, so that his words would not be heard as casual, as though he needed to make it understood that what he had to say was important for Woody to hear. He said he has been called a "hero" by many people in the aftermath of one harrowing day in New York City. But, he explained, it was the guys like my dad, the ones who—for days and weeks and endless months—didn't know if they would live or die in the fight for their country. The ones who did, and didn't, come back from war...*they,* he said, were the real heroes. "*You,*" he said pointedly, "you are the *real* hero."

My dad looked at him, a little too astonished to reach for the LightWRITER. He wouldn't have been able to anyway, because in the next instant the man pulled Woody close and embraced him for a long moment. When finally they separated, they were both in tears. The man looked again at Woody, embarrassed perhaps at such bottomless emotion—neither of them accustomed to such things. They smiled awkwardly at each other, and then fortunately, someone else nudged their way up to Woody to shake his hand. The firefighter quietly said, "Thanks." And moved off.

I don't know who he was. I doubt I'll ever know. But of those 17 flashing months I was able to spend with Woody, there was nothing more anyone could have said or done to honor him.

It was perfect.

While my dad was never a movie star or a senator, never famous, never rich; on that night—as one person after the next stepped up to thank him—he *was* a hero.

"In three words I can sum up everything I've learned about life: It goes on."

Robert Frost

Postscript

As I write these words, Woody has been gone more than a decade and a half. My trajectory in the years since his death was largely decided by one of our last conversations. I asked him if he had any regrets, assuming his answer would include marrying my mother (which usually gets a laugh when I say as much to friends). But, after he gave it some thought, he told me he wished he'd spent more time with me when I was small. It was odd, I thought, because he was around as much as anybody's dad in the '60s. Still, his comment made me look at my own life. It made me contrast the amount of time I was spending at the studio against the celerity of Henry and Joe's speeding childhoods. So—after working the next season on *The Drew Carey Show*, I told my agents I was going to take some time off, to spend it with the boys while they were still so young. As well, I wanted to write some things that were important to me.

In the years since, I have done exactly that.

And those two little boys who squealed and crawled onto Grampa's lap with their broken slot cars have moved out into the world. Henry graduated in the spring of 2019 from Puget Sound, near Seattle...with *two* degrees; one in Mathematics, one in Economics. Honors in both degrees. Magna Cum Laude. (Even still, he doesn't act like he's smarter than I.) He's now doing freelance software development for businesses in Washington. Joe graduated in the spring of 2019 from Kenyon College in Ohio with a degree in Economics. With honors. I'm extra proud of him for doing so well because I thought he was mostly just playing lacrosse. (And, btw, kicking ass.) After he did an internship the last summer before his senior year with an investment advisory firm in Santa Monica, he was asked to start as an associate there. (I look forward to many more conversations with him about his work that I won't understand.)

Most important, they both ended up decent, kind, conscientious human beings. And each with a razor sharp wit (of which I am often a victim).

Catherine is still teaching at a local high school, a job she endlessly enjoys. Our marriage admittedly suffered with the strain of so much that went on, but in the months and years that have since transpired, we have both done well in its repair. Marriage is at best a tricky business, an unlikely scenario in the context of being human. In the process of our evolving relationship, however, we renewed an affection for each other, discovered beyond all else, that we *like* each other.

Ted Danson? I won't even bother filling you in on him. Google. He's everywhere. When I learned that *Tuesdays with Ted* would be published, I emailed him and said that, if the book was moderately successful, "it could very well breathe new life into your flailing and misguided career. You're welcome."

He wrote back: "As usual you made me laugh... CONGRATULATIONS. Your angelic father must have connections. Ted."

My aunt Oleta moved back to Globe, Arizona shortly after Woody's death and, with the help of some money he left her, she was able to buy a new home. As I write this, she is 93 and no longer gets out of the house. Though, as her world has gotten smaller, she is still busy with a plethora of friends from her church, who (of course) adore her and drop by her house at a near constant rate to care for and visit her. She and I speak frequently and, each time we do, we express our love for each other. I was also heartened to learn that she hears from Jodi quite a bit these days.

Our friend Mary—who walked with Jodi and me the night Woody died—succumbed to cancer in the spring of 2019. During the six months of her illness, only one of our mutual friends knew her condition—something she was adamant about.

A few years ago, my brother read the manuscript of this book. He then sent me an email explaining that I would not be hearing from him again. I haven't and, after much thought, decided to let it be.

As I mentioned, in the days following my father's death, I drove to Walnut Creek in Northern California and visited the house we lived in at the foot of Mt. Diablo. Being there took me back to the fourth grade, when my best friend and I made virtual bombs out of spray paint cans and gasoline, and nearly burned down the neighborhood. That night, as I waited in my bedroom to learn my punishment, my dad came in and, after hearing the details and seeing my pallor, he patted my knee and said it looked like I'd already learned what I needed to learn. Then he got up and said good night.

I drove north from there to our house in Red Bluff, a small town, resting along the barren straights of the I-5, where we lived for a couple of years in the late '60s. An older couple was living there, Bill and Carol, and they were nice enough to let me poke around the place.

Though the house had been remodeled—my old bedroom had been turned into a hallway—it was still the same house, just more of it. As Carol and Bill took me through the living room, I stopped to look at the unchanged fireplace. Then I showed them a photo of me, at ten, sitting on my dad's lap in front of the same brickwork. In the picture, I was perhaps a little too big to be sitting on his lap, which may be what he was smiling about...or it could've been the early evening "highball" he was protecting with his free hand.

The kitchen had not changed, and it was there I stood by myself beside the yellow tile of the sink's countertop, just looking at it. The small chips in the tile, the contour of the grout between the tile, all of it unchanged since I last saw it at 13. And, in the quiet moments that Bill and Carol extended to me, I was determined to let its physical reality take me back in time.

In that kitchen, beside that sink, I remembered the many hours I stood beside the phone on the wall, dialing and redialing, in my efforts to have my voice heard on the town's only radio station, KBLF. (No such thing as "redial" back then...nor were there buttons! Just a clear plastic circle you stuck your finger in and rotated. *Real* dialing.) And on those rare occasions when I got through to the disk jockey to dedicate a song "on the air," I did so to Sally Wilson (the girl I wore my first tie for).

I remembered as well the moments of despair, the early warning signs of melancholy that would go unheeded, unchecked, that would simmer and later blossom into full-blown depression. I remembered the first of the assaults by my mother, when she would berate, belittle or scream venomous opprobrium at me or my father. And I remembered those moments when the tide of her emotions had ebbed, when I was in favor, when she taught me how to make clam dip for the holidays.

And then I remembered the evening my father came home from work in his standard stark white shirt and tie—and I, with a brand new bottle of "Red Disappearing Ink," decided to try it out on him. When he walked into the kitchen, I aimed the bottle, squeezed it and watched the stream of fake ink arc and splatter on the left breast of his white shirt. He looked down for a moment to study it. Then he looked up at me with, what would probably best be described as, significant incredulity. At that moment, he was clearly a man at a crossroads, unsure of exactly how to proceed, unsure of exactly which penalty to exact. And while the disappearing ink was "guaranteed to quickly fade," from my perspective, it was not doing so quickly enough. I stood frozen, holding a grin I was no longer sure about. And when finally the "ink" did fade away, I breathed again and showed him the bottle. He took it, looked it over and handed it back to me. He shook his head. "Russell T.," he said, "I thought you'd lost your cotton-picking mind."

The Spring after he died brought with it a desire to clean, to clear out, to move past the physical attachments. His house was filled still with the furniture that he brought with him from Pahrump, and those pieces he'd accumulated since moving to Studio City. After sorting through the potential keepsakes, I set about putting on a garage sale. In the process, I saw an opportunity to rid our own house of the ever-growing and encroaching collection of toddler toys; the blue and green and yellow plastic ephemera that choke and downgrade the overall value of any home and possibly its neighborhood. I presented the idea to Henry and Joe as something fun to do—the gathering up and selling of their respective stockpiles—a great way to make a little money of their own. The building of future entrepreneurs. Henry viewed the proposed scenario with predictable skepticism and then cynicism, ultimately deciding the venture was not worth his time or effort.

Joe, on the other hand, embraced it with zeal and began gathering a collection of broken and worthless belongings that would rival the contents of a dumpster behind the Salvation Army. He commandeered the deck in the back of Woody's house, establishing it exclusively for the sale of his toys. There they were carefully displayed, all of them—on chairs and benches and Woody's chaise lounge—along with a number of orphaned parts, pieces, the amputated arms and legs from other toys that had long since vanished.

As the first day of the sale began, I went around back to visit him, see how he was doing. He was gloriously optimistic about his prospects as he sat waiting for the unsuspecting to wander into his web. A few people had meandered through, but no sales yet. When I picked up a one-armed Buzz Lightyear with ink on his forehead, I began to understand why sales were lagging. He'd used a page of pre-printed price stickers that I'd run off on the computer. Everything was marked at $100 or more. Buzz Lightyear was $125.

"Joe," I said as delicately as I could, "I think your prices might be a little steep for some kids."

There was a restrained air of superiority to his tone when he explained to me, "The *kids* don't buy the stuff. Their *parents* do."

"Okay…" I said, still going gently, "but $125 for a broken Buzz Lightyear might be a little more than somebody's *parent* will want to pay."

"Why?"

"Well…because it's not worth it."

"Yeah, it is."

"No, it isn't."

"It is to me. I'd buy it."

"Joe, you don't have $125."

"Yeah, I do. You gave it to me."

"No. That was a quarter I gave you."

"Same thing," he said.

"How is that the same thing?"

"A quarter can be worth $125. If it's old."

"Yes. But the quarter I gave you was worth twenty-five cents."

"Oh."

"So, maybe you should lower your prices a little…"

"To what?"

"I don't know. Ten cents."

He thought about it a moment and finally shook his

head. "Nah. I'd rather have the $125."

By Fall, the house had been sold.

On the last day of escrow, Henry and I went over to double-check everything. We walked through the empty place one last time, checking the closets, the bathrooms, the kitchen shelves. As we stepped out onto the front porch, and I turned to lock the place up, I heard Henry, standing behind me, whisper quietly, "Good-bye, Grampa."

Woody's ashes stayed with us for a few months before they were sent to Oleta, so she could take them to Texas, as promised—where he was buried at the foot of his mother and father's graves. Before sending his ashes off, however, the boys and I took the box out to the back porch. We each grabbed a handful and put them in a small container of our own. A cigar box. After we did so, we took turns clapping out the dust over the side of the railing, watching the residue float out into the yard. Then we said our final good-byes to Grampa.

A few years later, my aunt called with news about my mother. As you may recall, the guy at the military cemetery in Nevada was in a bit of a quandary about what exactly to do with her ashes. The problem was that Woody had served "proudly as a sergeant in the U.S. Marine Corps, seeing action in the Pacific and European theatres of WWII..." and my mother hadn't. Out of curiosity one day, Oleta checked their website, and learned that Mary Woody apparently served proudly as a sergeant in the U.S. Marine Corps, having seen action in the Pacific and European theatres of WWII.

Unfortunately Woody's golf clubs—the ones I promised him I would use to pursue the game again—were stolen out of our garage a few years ago. It stung, but so much in this trip is about letting go. So, I let go. And then I bought some new clubs.

The cigar box with (our handfuls of) Woody's ashes now rests on the bookshelf in my office beside one of his old battered yellow flashlights, upon which worn black lettering says: "PROPERTY OF PACIFIC GAS & ELECTRIC." I'm pretty sure he "acquisitioned" it from PG&E sometime in the '60s. Its batteries, he probably put in there some 30 years ago. Still, when I shove the switch forward, its bulb slowly begins to glow. I like that.

Beside it, the LightWRITER. For a time, I kept it charged and working. But it is quiet now, in need of service. A few months after his death, I scrolled through its memory and played some of his saved messages.

Each still sounded like him. His voice.

Among the more poignant was a message he typed and saved to play for people who came by the house to look at his dog, Ace. This was after he came to realize it was time for him to give the dog away: "ACE LIKES TO BE COVERED WITH A BLANKET. I HAVE BEDDING AND TOYS YOU CAN HAVE."

And one I'd forgotten about. One he saved on the Saturday before he died. It was for Ted and Hattie Winston at *Becker*. "GIVE TED AND HATTIE A HUG FOR ME."

"MAKE SURE YOU FAIRAMOUNT TO JOE AND HENRY FOR THEIR SCHOOL." He'd made an obvious typo that, at first, I thought had something to do with Paramount. Then I realized it was missing the words,

"GIVE A" before "FAIRAMOUNT." He wanted to make sure that, of the money he'd leave behind, much of it went to Henry and Joe.

Of the myriad messages still on the LightWRITER, "T1" remains my favorite: "I LOVE YOU MY SON ALWAYS AND ALWAYS WILL."

When I was younger, time moved methodically, systematically, one tick after the next. These days, I look away from the clock for an instant and time has spun away like a meteor hurtling towards oblivion. I suppose there are ways to slow it down. Misery is one option. Joseph Heller's Lieutenant Dunbar (*Catch 22*) found a way of doing so by infusing his life with boredom and discomfort: "Dunbar loved shooting skeet because he hated every minute of it and the time passed so slowly."

Dunbar's solution aside, there isn't much to be done about time's increasing acceleration. As I've grown to see it, the only defense is a resolve to fill pieces of it with as much weight as possible. To that end; good friends, meaningful work, the passion to learn and the greedy consumption of moments with loved ones have become primary. For that perspective, I owe my father and the 17 months I spent with him.

To Henry and Joe, time has rendered Woody little more than a vague memory, having faded mostly to what is left of him in digital images. In the years following his death, the boys would pepper me with questions about him, both ridiculous and sublime. Like Joe's, when he asked about Woody having met certain people. Joe was maybe six at the time, and very disappointed with a great many of my responses; at one point insisting that I couldn't know with certainty that Grampa *never* met Abraham Lincoln.

"No, Joe, I'm pretty sure he didn't meet Abraham Lincoln."

"But you don't really know," he said with a wisp of patronization.

"Actually I do."

"No, you don't."

"Yes, I do."

He studied me suspiciously for a moment as though I had some political agenda in deceiving him. Then he said, "Well, I think maybe he did."

And Henry's $64,000 question when he asked why nobody could stop Woody's illness. The best I could do was shrug and say that some really smart people were trying to figure it out, but the human body is very complicated. It's hard to say why one person gets sick and another doesn't. But Grampa got to be a grandpa, *and* a grandpa to you. So he was luckier than most. I added, "And everyone ends up dying. Me. You. Everyone."

Because that's what life is.

And one day, I will fade from Henry and Joe's lives, and it will be their turn to feel what I felt when Woody faded from mine. Meanwhile, my love for him, and his expression of love for me, has made me want to spend as many minutes and hours as possible in Henry and Joe's company.

Absorbing.

A Short Note Regarding Henry and Joe

Each morning, before dropping one or both off at school, I told Henry and Joe three things they must do each day:

· *Learn a fact.*

· *Do some hard work (then have some fun).*

· *Be kind to someone who needs kindness.*

And that's who each has turned out to be.

I also told them many times—after I'd spent an evening on the back porch with one of several dear friends—that I hoped they would experience in their lives friendships as meaningful as those I have. What I didn't say was how much I hoped they would end up sharing that kind of friendship with each other.

As I write this, that has happened. On holidays, when we are all together, I see they truly enjoy each other's company. I see they like, love and respect each other. It is something that makes me feel that I have truly succeeded in my life.

"Everyone gets their rough day. No one gets a free ride. Today, so far, I had a good day. I got a dial tone."
Rodney Dangerfield

Photo Collection

Woody, circa 1965

Woody and Oleta in 1943 and 2001

My dad and brother at Woody's father's grave—where Woody was eventually buried

My mother and father

Woody with Joe, Henry (with the rabbit ears behind Woody)
and my bestfriend Craig's kids

Woody with Henry

Joe, me and Woody

Ted Danson and Woody

Cast & Crew of "Becker"

RUSS WOODY

Joe graduated from Kenyon College, Ohio May 2019. Henry and I were helping him move out, but decided to take a nap instead.

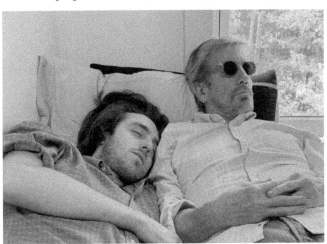

Regarding ALS and End of Life Issues

Amyotrophic lateral sclerosis afflicts 30,000 Americans every year. The ALS Association sponsors research and provides victims with vital services and supplies. If you'd like to make a donation, or if someone you know is suffering from this disease, please contact the ALS Association at: **alsa.org**

The services provided by Hospice caregivers are indispensable to those facing end of life issues.

To contact Hospice for help or to make a donation go to: **hospicenet.org**

Bibliography

Albom, Mitch. *Tuesdays with Morrie*. New York: Bantam Double-day Dell Publishing Group, Inc. 1997. Print.

Heller, Joseph. *Catch 22*. New York: Simon and Schuster. 1955. Print.

Hugo, Victor. *Les Miserables* . Harrisonburg: NAL Books. 1987. Print.

Kafka, Franz. *The Castle*. New York: Vintage Books/A Division of Random House/New York, NY, 1930. Print.

Rosenthal, Phil. *You're Lucky You're Funny*. New York: Viking Penguin, The Penguin Group (USA) Inc. 2006. Print.

Styron, William. *Darkness Visible; A Memoir of Madness*. New York: Random House. 1990. Print.

CPSIA information can be obtained
at www.ICGtesting.com
Printed in the USA
FSHW010332030819
60653FS